You Can Prophesy

Prophetic Principles, Protocols, and Procedures

"In the last days, God says, I will pour out my Spirit on all people. Your sons and daughters will prophesy, your young men will see visions, your old men will dream dreams." Acts 2:17

By Charmein T. Downer

xulon
PRESS

www.xulonpress.com

Charmein T. Downer
E-mail: chosen2beavessel@yahoo.com

Edited by Anna M. Walton

Acknowledgments:

ᐧᐧ

I wish to extend my personal and sincere thanks to:

First and foremost to my Heavenly Father. I love You with all my heart and I thank You for saving me, restoring me, and trusting me with the information in this book.

To my immediate family. Thanks for your endless support and confidence in me. I love you all very much.

To my spiritual parents. I have truly grown as a result of your Godly wisdom and love. Thank you for all your encouragement and teaching.

To my dear friend, Anna Walton. Thank you for your hard work in seeing this project completed.

My word shall sustain you for I have much work for you to do says the Lord. A woman of influence I have made you to teach and train my young women etiquette. Stay focused and in the secret place for I am your refuge says the Lord.

Prophetess Charnein

Table of Contents:

&&

Forward

ॐ

On November 5th, 2005, the Lord led me to Lansing, Michigan to do a Woman's Gathering called Alignment for the Assignment. During this time, Minister Charmein Downer's book, "You Can Prophesy" was introduced to me. I read it and loved it. I thought this book would be such a blessing to the women coming to the conference.

How ironic that God was aligning Charmein for her assignment that day. Many of her books sold to the women. Another process of her alignment was that she became a member of our local body, Lakeshore Int'l Family Training Center. Today, she is in a season where many doors have opened for her to teach, preach, and train in the prophetic.

I am blessed by Charmein's ability and anointing to write on the subject of prophecy with such clarity and simplicity. Her book, "You Can Prophesy," is a timely blessing to the Body of

Christ as God continues to spiritually shift many from fear to freedom, from religion to relationship, from spectators to participators with the Spirit of the living God.

Enjoy the simplistic, unpretentious, and interactive writings of Minister Charmein Downer. God is using her to equip the saints for the work of the ministry.

Prophetess Maria Hunter, Pastor
Lakeshore International Family Training Center

Chapter 1
You Can Hear His Voice

ঙ৹

It is true that all those that belong to the family of God can speak a prophetic message from the Lord. All flesh! That is what the Bible says. Not everyone will step out by faith and be used by God to speak a message to their neighbor, but this gifting has been made available to all that have translated from the Kingdom of darkness into the Kingdom of God.

> **"In the last days I will pour out my Spirit on all people. Your sons and daughters will prophesy, your young men will see visions and your old men will dream dreams. Even on my servants, both men and women, I will pour out my spirit in those days and they will prophesy"** **(Acts 2: 17,18).**

It is time for the children of God to know the things that have been freely given to us. Spiritual gifts and the ability to operate in supernatural manifestations by the leading of the Holy Spirit have been freely given to us, and it is a part of our inheritance.

> **"We have not received the Spirit of the world but the spirit that is from God, that we may understand what God has freely given us" (1 Corinthians 2: 12).**

Not only does God want us to know what is available to us, but also He has given us His Spirit to teach us that we may understand how to operate in spiritual acts and manifestations. The Lord desires to allow mankind to partner with Him in His endeavors in the earth. God is still looking for those who will mediate between heaven and earth and operate in spiritual dynamics so that He can intervene on man's behalf.

> **"I looked for a man among them who would build up the wall and stand before me in the gap on behalf of the land so I would not have to destroy it, but I found none" (Ezekiel 22: 30).**

If you feel like you are not qualified, wonderful! You are perfect for the Master's use.

> **"But God chose the foolish things of the world to shame the wise; God chose the weak things of the world to shame the strong. He chose the lowly things of this world and the despised things- and the**

things that are not to nullify the things that are, so that no one may boast before him" (1 Corinthians 1:27-29).

That settles it! You are the one that God is looking for to show Himself mighty in the earth. It is His desire that you hear His voice not only for yourself, but also to speak into the lives of those who can't hear because of their fallen state or because the cares of this world have choked the life out of their faith.

"We are therefore Christ ambassadors, as though God were making His appeal through us. We implore you on Christ behalf: Be reconciled to God" (2 Corinthians 1:27).

God wants to make His appeal through us. Our message, from whatever state an individual is in, is reconciliation. One of the main purposes for the prophetic ministry is to bring people into an intimate relationship with God for themselves.

"See I will send you the prophet Elijah before that great and dreadful day of the Lord comes. He will turn the hearts of the fathers to their children, and the hearts of the children to their fathers; or else I will come and strike the land with a curse" (Malachi 4: 5-6).

God is still concerned about His children and the land in which they live. He sent the Prophet with a Word in His mouth for reconciliation and restoration. We see in Malachi that God wants His people reconciled to one another and the land blessed and not cursed. The land is where God's people dwell and our resources come from the land. Our survival is based on the land we live in. In neighborhoods where the land is cursed and demonic reign is present, such as areas where drugs, prostitution, and poverty are prevalent, you will find a desperate need for reconciliation between God and man. The environment has had a tremendous effect upon many people. Because of the lack of "identity," some have fallen prey to the negative surroundings in which they live. For some people they do not see a way out and escaping their present circumstances seems impossible. The condition of God's people is heart breaking to the Lord because of the devastation of the effects of sin. But there is good news! God has called us as Ambassadors to bring reconciliation through prophetic evangelism to restore the relationship of those who have fallen away from the truth. We are to bring home prodigal sons and daughters. One prophetic Word from God can change the course of a person's life and set them on the path of destiny. The Bible says that prophecy is a sign for the believers, but we know it is the very heartbeat of God to reach the lost.

"Tongues then, are a sign, not for believers but for unbelievers; prophecy,

however, is for believers, not for unbelievers." (1 Corinthians 14:22)

"But if an unbeliever or someone
who does not understand comes in while
everyone is prophesying, he will be
convinced by all that he is a sinner and
will be judged by all, and the secrets of his
heart will be laid bare, So he will fall down
and worship God, exclaiming God is really
among you!" (1 Corinthians 14: 24, 25)

God Sees Two Ways:
1. Those who are in Christ.
2. Those who are lost.

The prophetic gifting is a valuable tool given to
the Body of Christ for the believers, but it is also
beneficial for unbelievers.

Receiving the Word of God

The Lord gave me an illustration once while I
was teaching the prophetic class at our church. He
said in order to collect the substance that exists upon
the moon we would need a vehicle, but that would
not be enough. Even if we could get the vehicle to
the moon by remote control, we still would need a
vessel (somebody) to get off of the ship and collect
the substance. Most importantly we need the fuel

that will allow the ship to be put in motion in the first place.

So it is with the prophetic, in order to get God's perspective, His heart, and His mind (thoughts) from Heaven to the natural realm we need a vehicle (prophecy), and then we would need fuel (faith), and finally a vessel (sons and daughters of the last days, Acts 2: 17). You were designed by God to hear His voice. Therefore, if you hear and recognize the voice of God, then you can deliver a message prophetically. Will you be one of the end-time vessels for the Master's use?

"Indeed all the prophets from Samuel on, as many as have spoken, have foretold these days. And you are heirs of the prophets and of the covenant God made with your fathers. He said to Abraham, 'through your offspring all peoples on earth will be blessed" (Acts 3: 24, 25).

Here we see again that God's purpose for mankind is for us to partner with Him, so that all people on earth can be blessed. In verse 24, we are called heirs of the prophets so guess what that means? You and I don't have to struggle with the thought, "Is the prophetic ministry for me?"

Yes! You are called by God to move in the prophetic gifts. Remember, you are an heir and heirs get to enjoy the goods left behind by their predecessors. The prophet Samuel changed the standard for all the other prophets that came behind him. In his days we see the school of the prophets, company of prophets, and the sons of the prophets (1 Samuel 10:10; 1 Kings 20:35; 2 Kings 2:3, 5). By the time the Prophet Joel arrived on the scene, God revealed to him that in the last days **"All Flesh!"** would prophesy.

> **"And afterward, I will pour out my spirit upon all flesh: and your sons and your daughters shall prophesy, your old men shall dream dreams, your young men shall see visions" (Joel 2:28).**

The Lord expanded the prophetic borders. Not only did the priest, prophets, sons, and company of prophets prophesy, but also the Lord foretold of the days that we are now living in. God is releasing a prophetic company of believers who will use the same creative power of words to shape their own destiny, as well as have an affect on everyone they influence.

Even while you are reading this book, today Joel 2:28 is being fulfilled in your lifetime. It does not take a rocket scientist to figure out that we are living in the last days. I have come to the conclusion that you can't exist in the earth without being someone's son or daughter. You are not excluded, nor exempt from this scripture if you are of human descent. So guess what, **You can prophesy!**

Don't miss out and don't let logic, doubt, and unbelief lock you out of what was freely given as a gift from God to you. The Apostle Paul reminded

Timothy not to neglect the gift that was given to benefit the Body of Christ, and neither should we.

"Don't neglect your gift that was given to you through a prophetic message when the body of elders laid their hands on you" (1Timothy 4:14).

This scripture is still speaking volumes to us today. The Word says, today if you hear My voice harden not your heart. I encourage you to open up your heart and receive the infallible truths in the Word of God concerning the prophetic. This truth will only become real to you if you embrace it and mix it with faith.

"For we also had the Gospel preached to us, just as they did; but the message they heard was of no value to them, because those who heard it did not combine it with faith" (Hebrews 4:2).

We are told not to neglect the gifts that have been made available to us. God has released teachers within the Body of Christ to bring clarity and understanding so that we would not perish for the lack of knowledge in all areas of our Christian walk. The information in this book will have no value to you if it is not mixed with faith. Faith is a word that is marked by action. Will you still go to heaven if you don't prophesy? Of course, but you just won't fulfill the words spoken in 1 Peter 1:10 while here on earth.

"Each one should use whatever gift he has received to serve others, faithfully administering God's grace in its various forms" (1Peter 1:10).

Jesus said that He came that we may have the abundance of all that life as a child of God has to offer. The prophetic gift is a part of our inheritance and has the creative ability to release the abundance that Jesus was referring to when He made this promise. We are not just flesh and blood. We are supernatural beings; we are Spirit, we have a soul, and we live in an earth suit we refer to as our bodies. We are packed with power and authority. We are to subdue, rule, and have dominion, but we first must obtain identity. Then, the Holy Spirit will bring to our awareness what has already been made available to us to be effective in advancing the Kingdom of God.

If you don't understand the prophetic gift, stay open and the Holy Spirit will lead you and guide you into all truth. A closed heart is like a closed hand. Take a moment and make a fist with your palms facing upward. You will discover that you can't get anything out, but you also can't receive anything either. Open up your heart and allow the Holy Spirit to lead you and guide you into all truth.

"The man without the spirit does not accept the things that come from the Spirit of God, for they are foolishness to him, and he cannot understand them,

**because they are spiritually discerned"
(1 Corinthians 2:14).**

Take a moment and speak this prophetic prayer over
your life.

*"I demolish arguments and every preten-
sion that exalts itself up against the knowledge of God. I take authority over thoughts
from the enemy and every ignorant and
mind blocking spirit. I take you captive
and command you to be bound and make
you obedient to Christ. I loose myself from
ignorance, tradition, and religious practices
that have no value. I command blinders to
fall off of my spiritual eyes that I may know
the truth and be set free from ignorance. I
loose myself from every idea and opinion
embedded in me that does not line up with
the Word of truth. I receive the Word, I
believe the Word, I am a son/daughter of the
promise, I live in the last days, therefore I
can and will prophesy the Word of the Lord"
(Matthew 18:18, 2 Corinthians 10:35).*

*"Father according to Ephesians 1:17
&18, let this scripture be activated in the lives
of those who embrace the revelation written
in this book. I pray that You would release
the Spirit of wisdom and revelation that we
may know who we are as children of God.
Teach us how to operate and cooperate with*

You, that Your will may be done through us as vessels on earth as it is in heaven. Let the eyes of our understanding be enlightened, that we may know what is the hope that You have in us as saints to be end-time warriors, and not just passive pew members. Teach us how to be champions for our region, taking all spirits captive and making them obedient to Jesus Christ. Allow us to walk in the fullness of submission and obedience as we present ourselves as living sacrifices Holy and acceptable unto You while we are here in the earth. In Jesus' name I pray, amen."

The Children of God Are Heirs of Salvation and Can Prophesy

This is the generation that can and will move in the prophetic ministry. Those that are the sons of God can hear His voice. What child does not recognize the voice of their parent? If my mother called me on the phone, I do not have to ask who is speaking. I recognize her voice based on years of communication and fellowship that I have encountered through an intimate relationship with her.

So it is with the Father. The more time you spend with Him, the finer the line becomes between distinguishing your voice from His voice. The distinction becomes very clear after you've spent countless hours of intimate time in His presence through prayer, praise, worship, and meditation of His Word.

When the prophetic ministry was not popular in the Christian sector in my region, I persevered and now I am elated to see with my own eyes the transformation of many lives by the Glory of God as they learn to hear the voice of God for themselves. It is rewarding to see people develop a personal relationship with God and put no idols before Him. The Lord is restoring this gift back to the Body of Christ. This is not the Old Testament where He spoke through the Prophets and Priest only. God is talking in a today-generation voice. He is speaking to all His people because we are living in the last days.

"Now if we are children, then we are heirs- heirs of God and co-heirs with Christ, if indeed we share in his sufferings in order that we may share in his glory" (Romans 8:17).

You have to have a clear understanding of the word heir and co-heir to appreciate what this passage is saying. I found in Webster's dictionary that an heir is one who inherits, or is entitled to succeed to a hereditary rank, title or office. It also can be one who receives some endowment or quality from a parent or predecessor. Hearing this revelation definitely makes my spirit leap for joy because God said that we are heirs and co-heirs. What He is really saying is that there is a portion that I have given you as My children, but that is not where the blessings end. Not only do you have a portion as an heir, but also you have a double portion because He said we are **heirs of God and co-heirs with Christ!**

We will get what is coming to us from the Father. In addition, we get to walk in all that Jesus walked in and left for us at His departure after His death and resurrection (John 14:12). Now that is enough for you to put this book down and shout hallelujah and thank You, Jesus! Receiving a double portion is an awesome thought.

> **"Because you are sons, God sent the Spirit of his Son into our hearts, the Spirit who calls out, "Abba Father." So you are no longer a slave, but a son: and since you are a son, God has made you also an heir"** **(Gal 4: 6, 7).**

Every demon in hell is afraid of you getting this information and walking in the truth of this scripture, because they know without the identity of who you are, and identifying with what is in you, and what has been made available to you that you are limited.

> **"What I am saying is that as long as the heir is a child he is no different from a slave, although he owns the whole estate"** **(Galatians 4:1).**

Although you have access to all this knowledge, you will only use what you already know, under-stand, embrace, and believe.

"By wisdom a house is built, and through understanding it is established; through knowledge its rooms are filled with rare and beautiful treasures" **(Proverbs 24: 3, 4).**

I encourage you to let your house be established with understanding of the prophetic gift that has been made available for you as a part of your inheritance. Fill your rooms with knowledge from your study time in this particular area. If God were to come and visit your home, would He want to live in the house that you have built?

"Don't you know that you yourselves are God's temple and that God's Spirit lives in you" **(1 Corinthians 3:16)?**

Are there any articles inside of you that would be familiar to Him and make Him feel like He was at home, so He could get comfortable? I don't want Him to just visit from time to time. This would mean that He would come and go. I want to make my temple a place of habitation for the Lord.

"Do you not know that your body is a temple of the Holy Spirit, who is in you, whom you have received from God? You are not your own; you were bought at a price. Therefore honor God with your body" **(1 Corinthians 6: 19, 20).**

**"What agreement is there between
the temple of God and idols? For we are
the temple of the living God. As God has
said: I will live with them and walk among
them, and I will be their God, and they will
be my people" (2 Corinthians 6:16).**

I determined long ago to embrace and believe that
I can do and be all that the Bible says I can be. I am
a living witness that the prophetic ministry is real.
It changes lives and it is a part of every believer's
destiny. It is intertwined within your genetic structure
to hear God's voice. You were born with the ability to
communicate with your creator (Psalms 139: 1-18).
This means not only to receive a prophetic Word, but
we have been commissioned by God as Ambassadors
to speak prophetically. We are representatives for the
Kingdom of God.

**"We are therefore Christ ambassa-
dors, as though he were making His appeal
through us" (2 Corinthians 5:20).**

We all are called to represent the Kingdom of
God. Ambassadors are sent to other countries because
the president can't be everywhere at all times. They
conduct business on behalf of their country. God is
raising up a prophetic company of believers with an
apostolic anointing sent to go forth in demonstration
and power. He wants to make His appeal in the earth
through you. Not only did we as children of God
inherit the blessings of our forefathers, but we also

inherited the responsibilities to carry on the plans of our God. Are you an heir to the throne? If so, then allow God to show you what has been left for you as a part of your inheritance.

> **"Because you are sons, God has sent the Spirit of His son into our hearts, the Spirit who calls out, 'Abba – Father'. So you are no longer a slave, but a son and since you are a son, God has made you also an heir" (Galatians 4:1-5).**

As children of God and co-heirs with Christ, it is important to be aware of our inheritance and full rights as sons and daughters of God, or else you will become a product of this scripture. There are some things that legally belong to you. It is written in the living testament of the will left by Jesus. Prophecy is one of the inherited things (John 16:12-14). Through prophetic writings and Rhema words, God reveals what is hidden for us.

> **"At this time Jesus, full of joy through the Holy Spirit, said, "I praise you, father, Lord of Heaven and earth, because you have hidden these things from the wise and learned, and revealed them to little children. Yes, Father, for this was your good pleasure" (Luke 10:21).**

If you are not aware of what is in the estate then you will not take advantage of your rights to the inheritance. As long as you stay in an infantile or childish state spiritually, you will be subject to guardians and trustees assigned to guard and protect what is rightfully yours.

"We have much to say about this (the prophetic), but it is hard to explain because you are slow to learn. In fact, though by this time you ought to be teachers, you need someone to teach you the elementary truths of God's word all over again. You need milk, not solid food" (Hebrews 5:11, 12).

Confession,
I commit to advance in my spiritual development. I will not be stagnated or become a spiritual midget taken captive and placed under arrested development by the basic principles of this world. I will grow and move beyond the elementary teaching listed in Hebrews 6:1,2 and go on to maturity. I am spiritual as well as a physical being, and I will take advantage of what God has redeemed for me through His son Jesus, my savior and Lord. I will receive the full right of what is mine as a son/daughter of the most High God.

The things that are hidden and not disclosed are our inheritance to receive through revelation. It is important that you understand that the prophetic ministry is not just about giving someone a prophetic Word. It is the vehicle that God uses to get the revelation from heaven into the earth concerning your life, as well as others.

"For I know the thoughts that I think towards you, sayeth the Lord, thoughts of peace, and not of evil, to give you an expected end" (Jeremiah 29:11 KJ).

"... From now on I will tell you of new things, of hidden things unknown to you" (Isaiah 48: 6).

"I am the Lord; that is my name! I will not give my glory to another or my praise to idols. See the former things have taken place, and new things I declare; before they spring into being I announce them to you" (Isaiah 42: 8,9).

God is still revealing His plans, and His will through the prophetic voices of today. No man can exclude us from operating in the prophetic gift because it does not come by the will of man.

"For prophecy never had its origin in the will of man, but men spoke from God as they were carried along by the Holy Spirit" (1 Peter 1: 21).

It is not the decision of man if you can or cannot prophesy. God said you could because He has poured out His Spirit upon the earth for this very cause; that all sons and daughters, servants and menservants can speak prophetically Words of exhortation, edification, and comfort. God wants to reveal the hidden secrets of Heaven to you as well as through you. **The only one that can stop you- is you!**

Those That Are Saved Can Hear the Voice of God

Anyone that is connected or has been reconciled through the gift of salvation to the Father can hear the voice of God, and therefore fulfill the commission on their lives to be ministers of reconciliation.

"Therefore, if anyone is in Christ, he is a new creation; the old has gone, the new has come! All this is from God, who reconciled us to himself through Christ and gave us the ministry of reconciliation; that God was reconciling the world to himself in Christ, not counting men's sins against them. And he has committed to us the message of reconciliation. We are therefore Christ's Ambassadors, as though God were making his appeal through us. We implore you on Christ's behalf: Be reconciled to God" (2 Corinthians 5: 17).

Our prophetic destiny is to reconcile people to God. This is the ministry that we have been entrusted with and we see by this scripture that God wants to make His appeal through us. We are called by God to use this gift. Will everyone use it? Probably not, but the important thing to remember is many are called, but few are chosen. The real question is: are you willing to position yourself to be chosen by God to be used in the prophetic gifting?

There is so much more to salvation and many of us do not walk in the fullness of what has been made available to us. The disciples at Corinth, like many Christians today, received the plan of salvation and stopped there. The Apostle Paul challenged the believers to go further and walk in the power and demonstration of God.

"While Apollos was at Corinth, Paul took the road through the interior and arrived at Ephesus. There he found some disciples and asked them, "Did you receive the Holy Spirit when you believed?" They answered, No, we have not even heard that there is a Holy Spirit." So Paul asked what baptism you received?" "John's baptism," they replied. Paul said, "John's baptism was a baptism of repentance. He told the people to believe in the one coming after him, that is, in Jesus." On hearing this, they were baptized into the name of the Lord Jesus. When Paul placed His hands on them, the Holy Spirit came upon them,

and they spoke in tongues and prophesied"
(Acts 19: 1-7).

If you embrace this information as truth and apply it to your life, then by faith you shall move in the prophetic gifting. In the Old Testament, the Lord only entrusted a few with His plans.

"Surely the sovereign Lord does nothing without revealing His plans to his servants the prophets" (Amos 3:7).

Jesus, however, set a new precedent and a new order into effect (Heb. 9:15, 10:19, 12:24). This new order took us from a place of servant hood, only taking orders and never being allowed to form an intimate relationship to becoming friends with God.

"I no longer call you servants, because a servant does not know his master's business. Instead I have called you friends, for everything that I have learned from my Father I have made known to you" (John 15:15).

As friends of God it is His desire to share the Father's business with us. He doesn't want us left out in the dark with little to no information concerning our lives, and the lives of those we are destined to influence day to day. The Lord desires to speak to us face to face as friends in the same way that He did with Moses (Exodus 33:11). We must become intimate and cultivate a personal relationship with our Creator. It is time for all believers to know and embrace our destiny as a prophetic generation.

In the movie The Lion King, Mufasa was the head of the tribe. His son Simba was born to lead his generation and take over when his father died. Simba was destined to be the heir to the throne. He witnessed his father's death and it was a traumatic event. He linked up with two characters that were heathens. They had no godly wisdom to impart into him. He developed their view of life "Hakuna Matata", which was their problem free philosophy. No matter what happened they lived a worry free life. One day Nala, who was Simba's childhood friend, discovered that Simba was alive. She beckoned him to take his rightful position as heir to the throne. She wanted him to set order to the chaos that his uncle Scar had created while ruling in his stead. He refused, but the monkey "Rafiki" went to Him and gave him godly counsel. He reminded him of his roots, where he had come from, and what he was destined to be. My favorite line of the movie was when Rafiki told Simba, "You are more than what you have become". I am telling you now, if you are saved and you do not have miracles, signs and wonders that accompany the gifts of the Spirit following you as a believer, then you are more than what you have become (Mark 16: 17, 18).

Chapter 2
Moses and Paul wished all would prophesy

ഐ

According to scripture, Moses was one of the most humble men on earth (Numbers 12:3). Moses tapped into the revelation of intimacy with God by having a personal relationship with Him. While his peers where in bondage through slavery by the Egyptians, the Lord chose him as the deliverer. He fulfilled and completed his mission to deliver the Israelites from the hands of Pharaoh, however he didn't stop there. It was his desire to see all men experience the voice of God through intimacy with the Heavenly Father.

"But Moses replied, "Are you jealous for my sake? I wish that all the Lord's people were prophets and that the Lord would put His Spirit on them" (Numbers 11:29).

Moses set up the tent of meeting for anyone that wanted to hear from God (Exodus 33:7-11). The Lord wants to speak to us as friends, so all we have to do is pitch a tent and wait for him to respond. The time for the one-man show is over. God is moving by His Spirit upon the earth and as my leader always says, "He will use a prepared vessel."

"It was he who gave the apostle, prophet, pastor, teacher, and evangelists to prepare God's people for works of service, so that the body of Christ may be built up" (Ephesians 4:11, 12).

If you are submitted to a local church, then your pastor and leadership should fit into one of these five governmental callings instituted by God for His church. Your local church should be training you to do the work of the ministry. The work of the ministry is outside as well as inside of the walls of the church building. The key is you must learn to use the tools that come with the job in order to complete the assignment that God has given us individually, as well as corporately. There are many tools given to the Body, but we use them according to the job. Prophecy is one of the tools given by God to be used in the Body of Christ.

We are prophetic people and have been since birth. We are like a radio with a transistor. It doesn't matter what room you put a radio in, or where you are at geographically. As long as you have batteries or a plug, the transistor within the radio can pick up the sound waves that we can't see with the naked eye.

Likewise, we as children of God, made in the image of God, also have a built in transistor. This is our spirits. We are fearfully and wonderfully made and we can connect with the voice of God anytime and anywhere because it is a part of our genetic makeup. We have been destined by design to hear the voice of God.

When I came into the knowledge of the prophetic gifting, I asked God why He didn't speak to me when I was a teenager getting involved in trouble-some situations. He said, "I did and I always have because I have your best interest at heart". I replied, "No, you didn't." He responded by saying, "Oh, yes I did." Then He brought back to my remembrance when I would do something that was disorderly, and had to pay consequences for my actions. One of the first thoughts that came to my mind was, "I should have went with my first mind, or something told me not to do that, or to go the other direction."

The Lord showed me that this was an example of Him speaking to me and trying to redirect me. However, because of sin, rebellion, or my own lustful desires, my will would override or shut down the voice of God speaking through my conscience.

Our lack of training on how to be sensitive to God's Spirit when He speaks is usually cancelled out by our own reasoning. If you take a moment and think back you would see that what the world calls intuition (knowing something without prior infor-mation) is actually the prophetic gift in operation by way of a Word of knowledge. A Word of knowledge is the supernatural ability to know something that you could not have possibly known naturally (1 Corinthians 12:8).

We are more aware and in tune with the carnal portion of our makeup as humans, but God intricately designed our spirits in His image and likeness. Could you imagine a computer designer building a computer that he could not interact with, give commands to, and get a response? We were created by God to interact with Him. God created the living creatures in Genesis just as He created man. The difference was that God said He wanted man to look like Him (Genesis 1:26,27). There was also something special that was given to man that set them above and apart from the living creatures that God made. God blew the breath of life into man in the beginning (Genesis 2:7). After the fallen state of man, God's Spirit does not reside inside of us until we accept the gift of salvation.

"Again Jesus said, "Peace be with you! As the father has sent me, I am sending you." And with that he breathed on them and said, "Receive the holy Spirit..." (John 20:21, 22).

"Peter replied, "Repent and be baptized, every one of you, in the name of Jesus Christ for the forgiveness of your sins. And you will receive the gift of the Holy Spirit" (Acts 2:38).

"While Apollos was at Corinth, Paul took the road through the interior and arrived at Ephesus. There he found some disciples and asked them, "Did you receive the Holy Spirit when you believed?" They answered, "No, we have not even heard that there is a Holy Spirit. When Paul placed his hands on them, the Holy Spirit came on them, and they spoke in tongues and prophesied" (Acts 19:1, 2, 6).

This world system is easy to be conformed to, but we are told to transform our minds. The pattern of our thinking and understanding concerning the spiritual gifts must be transformed. When we are ignorant concerning spiritual gifts our transistors pick up a lot of static, but through anointed teaching God can tune you in to the right channel that you may become aware of the fact that you can hear the voice of God. If you can hear His voice, then you are qualified as an Ambassador to deliver a message, so therefore, "You can prophesy."

Lets say I want to build a house. I would need a foreman to oversee the workers. In order to get the best results I would also need a skilled team. I would need an architect for the blue prints, a plumber for the piping system, a painter and interior designer for decorating, and an electrician for the electrical system and so forth.

The overall goal is to establish a structure that someone can comfortably live in and make it their home. Each person hired has a job to do and they also have different tools that are required to get their portion of the job completed. So it is with the Body of Christ. If I go to the Hospital to visit the sick, I need the gift of faith to lay hands for healing or maybe even a miracle. If someone needs to be delivered, then I need the gift of discerning of spirits to know what spirit I am dealing with. If God wants to get a message delivered, then as an Ambassador and representative for the Kingdom of God, I will need the gift of prophecy to speak God's will. Prophecy is one of the gifts of the Spirit that is profitable to all.

"There are different kinds of gifts, but the same Spirit. There are different kinds of service, but the same Lord. There are different kinds of working, but the same God works all of them in all men. Now to each one the manifestation of the Spirit is given for the common good" (1 Corinthians 12: 4-7).

"Study to show thyself approved unto God, a workman that needeth not to be ashamed, rightly dividing the word of truth" (2 Timothy 2:15).

There are three things that we need to examine closely to understand this passage of scripture pertaining to the prophetic gifting:

1. Study to Show Thyself Approved

According to Webster's dictionary, to study means to devote oneself, something attracting close attention or examination, and a person who learns and memorizes something. God wants us to devote ourselves to learning all we need to know about everything in the Bible including, not excluding the gifts of the Spirit. **"Now about spiritual gifts, brothers I do not want you to be ignorant" (1 Corinthians 12:1).**

2. A Workman That Does Not Need to be Ashamed

You don't have to be ashamed when you understand what to do, how to do, and when the Holy Spirit comes to move among the people and He chooses you to move through. It is shameful to see the presence of God in a service and He wants to speak, heal, or deliver His people, and the people have been so conditioned that all they do is buck and shout when they feel His presence. It also is shameful when the Holy Spirit enters in and no one knows how to yield that He may move upon His people. **"My people are destroyed from lack of knowledge..." (Hosea 4:6).** When God pours out His spirit it is for a reason. There is a purpose for everything God does. **"In the last days I will pour out my Spirit on all people. Your sons and daughters will prophesy" (Acts 2:17).**

3.   Rightly Divide the Word of Truth

If God allowed this to be written in the Word, then obviously there have been some misinterpretations and teachings that were wrong. I encourage you when you sit under any preacher or teacher honor them and honor the Word, but please study for yourself. **"Dear friends, do not believe every spirit, but tests the spirits to see whether they are from God, because many false prophets have gone out into the world"** (**1 John 4:1**). Don't just be satisfied with a humanistic interpretation of scripture, but allow the Holy Spirit to give you true revelation concerning the scripture. Who better to ask than the very Author of the work? **"Above all you must understand that no prophecy of Scripture came about by the prophets own interpretation. For prophecy never had its origin in the will of man, but men spoke from God as they were carried along by the Holy Spirit"** (**1 Peter 1:20, 21**).

When you study and devote yourself to understanding, knowledge is gained. For example, engineers study engineering and when it is time to look for a job they are chosen because of their ability to be effective and efficient in that particular area. If an engineer were needed, you wouldn't look for a professional basketball player to get the job done. Why? Because the ball player has studied, practiced, and mastered the skill of playing ball. A professional basketball player would not be able to give you the details and skills needed to get your project done from an engineers' point of view. They can only give according to their ability. You would have to hire an engineer, because that is his skill and trade. Skill is based on ability and experience. Ability and experience is based on the knowledge one has acquired to accomplish a task.

When the Lord gets ready to move in a particular area, He looks for those who are open, who understand the dynamics of this gift through their study, and can rightly divide between self and the voice of God. You are open to the manifestations and the gifts of God when you believe. Most of us, because of human nature, only believe what we can see or comprehend and the Lord knows this. That is why He tells us not to reject prophecy, but to test it.

"Do not put out the Spirit's fire; do not treat prophecies with contempt. Test everything. Hold on to the good"
(1 Thessalonians. 5: 19-21).

"Do not smother the Holy Spirit. Do not scoff at those who prophesy, but test everything that is said to be sure it is true, and if it is, then accept it"
(1 Thessalonians 5: 19-22 Living Bible).

When the Lord wants to release a prophetic Word into the earth or an individual's life, He chooses those whom He approves.

"Then I heard the voice of the Lord saying, "Whom shall I send? And whom will go for us?" And I said, "Here am I. Send me!"(Isaiah 6:8).

He looks to use mankind in His endeavors, but He searches for those who have applied their heart to get wisdom and in all their getting to get an understanding. Our Heavenly Father is looking for yielded vessels that are willing to be used in whatever capacity He so desires. Many of us can believe God to preach and pray and walk in prosperity, but why won't the Body of Christ believe to prophesy, lay hands on the sick, and cast out devils? Walking in the miraculous signs and power of God is included in our mandate (Mark 16:17, 18).

This is the exciting part of ministry; this is how the gates of hell will not prevail against the church. We are not just weak humans who have to suffer through the attacks of the enemy. We are power-packed supernatural beings created by God to rule and have dominion in the earth. We are called to subdue and we have the supernatural gifts to assist us in our God-given task. God can send His word through this book and it will accomplish what He sent it to do, and it will not return unto Him void. The Holy Spirit is quickening many of you right now as you read the pages of this book as knowledge and understanding floods your hearts and minds. **I command the prophetic gifting that is on the inside of you to be stirred up and activated right now according to the measure of faith within you in Jesus' name, amen.**

Some people are comfortable and satisfied with the church experience. They go to church, hear the sermon, and go home to start the process all over again. However, when I took hold of the revelation in Acts 2:17, 18, I ran and told everyone that would listen. Like King David, I had the mindset to tell God that, "I hate what He hates and I love what He loves." I loathe with passion ignorance, because it causes many of the people of God to miss out on the abundance of life that Jesus made available for us.

I pray that you will not let the enemy trick you into living your entire life without identity and not discovering your purpose in the earth. Also, I encourage you to find out what gifts God has placed inside of you to accompany you in fulfilling your destiny.

It is important for you to know your purpose and destiny in the earth. You must realize there are supernatural gifts within you waiting to be liberated, activated, and stirred up so you can walk in all that God has called you to do. **"But we have this awesome treasure in jars of clay to show that this all- surpassing power is from God and not from us" (2 Corinthians 4:8).**

In my time of study the Lord revealed to me there were three platforms that I know of that would activate the gifts within a believer. There may be more, but this is the revelation God gave to me.

1. Knowledge
   You can't do something if you have no awareness or understanding of its existence,

or teaching on how to properly function in a specific area.

2. <u>Laying on of Hands</u>
   In this case we would call this impartation. It is a physical action as a point of contact as the Holy Spirit causes what lies dormant within a believer to become active (Acts 19:5, 6).

3. <u>Prophetic Word</u>
   A prophetic Word spoken over an individual or group of people can cause life to come to dead and dry things (Ezekiel 37: 4,5). The prophetic Words can also call forth gifts and callings (1Timothy 4:14).

One of the biggest wiles of the enemy is to keep the Body of Christ out of the knowledge of their God-given authority and what has been made available to the saints. The prophet Isaiah had issues like us, (he fell into idolatry) but God still used him.

"In the year THAT king Uzziah died, I saw the Lord seated on a throne, high and exalted, and the train of His robe filled the temple" (Isaiah 6:1).

Isaiah was a prophet before Uzziah died, yet because of his love and adoration for the king it was not until he was removed that he saw the Lord, in verse 5 of the same chapter, he says that he is a man of unclean lips. Nevertheless, he responds to the call because God wants to send His Word to the people. Today God is still looking for those who will move in the prophetic gifting and be a blessing to His people. We can all identify with Isaiah the prophet. All of the words that come out of our mouths are not always pleasing to God. The unsaved people that we live among also have unclean lips. The same God that sent the angels with the coals to touch Isaiah's lips can send angels to touch our lips, and take away the guilt and sin and make us worthy to go and speak the messages of God. The Apostle Peter encourages us to faithfully use the gifts we have received to serve others.

"Each one should use whatever gift he has received to serve others, faithfully administering God's grace in its various forms. If anyone speaks, he should do it as one speaking the very words of God" (1 Peter 4:10, 11).

The Apostle Paul wished that all would operate in the gift of prophecy.

"He who speaks in a tongue edifies himself, but he who prophesies edifies the church. I would like every one of you to speak in tongues, but I would rather have you prophesy. He who prophesies is greater than one who speaks in tongues, unless he interprets, so that the church may be edified" (1 Corinthians 14: 4, 5).

The church is edified when prophecy goes forth. We are encouraged to excel in gifts that build. **"So it is with you, since you are eager to have spiritual gifts, try to excel in gifts that build up the church" (1 Corinthians 14: 12).**

All who belong to the family of God are encouraged to operate in spiritual gifts. If no one ever told you before, I am telling you that you are important and you matter. The Body is a unit and made up of many parts. We need your part to function effectively in ministering, because we prophesy in part. Therefore, my part alone is not enough. It takes team effort to get the job done.

You are equipped to move in everything that the Bible talks about. I am writing this book because I believe the Word of God. The most important scripture that I embraced was that God is not a respecter of persons. If the ordinary, everyday people in the Bible could do it and they didn't have technology and the resources available to them that we have today, then I know I can do it, especially if the Word says it has been made available to me. I used to be a daredevil in the world. Why would I become passive now that I'm in the Kingdom of God?

The Kingdom of God is still suffering violence, so God is raising up warriors that will take everything back from the enemy by force. I will use that same tenacity and fighting, aggressive spirit that I had in the world to combat the forces of darkness with whatever tools God has given me to possess the land and all that were lost by our forefathers. The enemy has tried to rob the Body of Christ of this awesome gift by blinding the eyes of baby Christians, and lying to the saint by making them believe the gifts were only for the elite or those who hold a title in the church. As a spiritual enforcer of the laws of God's Kingdom, because I am apostolic and sent by God, I am here to tell you that is a lie from the pit of hell. **All flesh can prophesy!** You are important and the power of life and death resides in your tongue as a believer. The people of God used to run to the priests and prophets to inquire of the Lord for direction and information. This is still available to us today, but it is important that you know you can hear the voice of the Lord for yourself as a royal priesthood (1 Peter 2:9). There is safety in the multitude of counselors, but we must always go to the Lord first. God is a jealous God and we should set no idols before Him. You must learn to discern the voice of the Lord for yourself.

"Follow the way of love and eagerly desire spiritual gifts, especially the gift of prophecy"(1 Corinthians 14: 1).

Eagerly desire spiritual gifts! We desire a lot of things, but this particular scripture tells us to desire spiritual gifts. We desire prosperity, some desire to find favor with their leaders, some desire promotion, or even materials things. We are told not just to desire, but also to **eagerly** desire spiritual gifts. This is not the teaching you would normally hear on a Sunday morning in some churches, but it is scriptural.

Jeremiah was afraid when the Lord revealed to him that He wanted him to be His spokesman. **"Ah sovereign Lord I do not know how to speak; I am only a child." But the lord said to me do not say I am only a child.' You must go to every one I send you to and say whatever I command you"** **(Jeremiah 1:6, 7).** The Lord said in the last days He would pour out His Spirit upon all flesh and sons and daughters would prophesy. It was not just a cute statement made because He needed to fill up some empty space in the pages of the Bible. It was for this very reason; He wants to send you with a Word in your mouth that will cause change to some, direction to many, and understanding to others.

This is the big picture: God wants you to be a well-rounded vessel not lacking in anything (Romans 1:11). Spiritual gifts make us strong and as believers we should know how to operate in the gifts of the Spirit, so we can be used by God to strengthen others. As the world says, "If you don't know you better ask somebody."

"Now about spiritual gifts brothers, I do not want you to be ignorant" (1 Corinthians 12:1).

Whatever you do if you take time to read information and spend your money for the information then put this in your spiritual archive. Information without application is useless. **"In the same way, faith by itself, if it is not accompanied by action, is dead" (James 2:17).** Most people will not embrace what they don't comprehend, so if you do not understand then set your hearts like Solomon in Ecclesiastes to seek out wisdom and search out this matter. Please do not show contempt for prophecy as 1 Thessalonians 5:19 warns us.

The Lord wants you to know that you are a part of the generation that He has chosen. In our days, the last days, God is pouring out His Spirit upon His people. It is our destiny to be sent by God with boldness and understanding to be used to deliver a life-giving and life-changing Word to the masses. When God sends a Word it can be through the Rhema (spoken) Word of God, or the Logos (written) Word of God. Whichever way He desires to send His Word and through whom is totally up to our Heavenly Father.

Why does God use some in the prophetic dimension opposed to others? When we limit ourselves through our ability to yield to His will, we limit the possibility of God manifesting His will through us as He touches others. Most of us will not yield to what we don't understand. This is why we have to take responsibility for our own growth. You are your greatest influence. No matter what others teach, preach, or say, you are ultimately the one that decides what you will embrace or reject. You must study for yourself if you want God's approval upon your life.

God approves of those who will yield and have set their hearts to understanding. When God wants to use someone to deliver a prophetic message, He takes into account those who He knows understands what He wants to do and how to operate in whatever dimension He wants to move in.

"The eyes of the Lord keep watch over knowledge, but He frustrates the words of the unfaithful" (Proverbs 22:12).

The truth is He uses those who are willing to yield themselves to Him, but the fact of the matter is very few people are willing to yield when there is a lack of understanding in how to function in the gifts of the Spirit and how important they are. If you had a message that you wanted delivered within a certain time frame and you had the option to use someone, whom would you choose? The messenger that says I have not been there before, and I'm not familiar with the territory, but I'm willing, or I have never been that way before and I refuse to go there because I'm not familiar with the territory. Most likely the one that is willing is a lot easier to work with because they are open and teachable.

If you compare a mule's ability to a horse's, it's a no-brainer. When a job needs to be done, time is of the essence, because one Word from God through a messenger can change the course of someone's life. God gives grace to the humble and he resists the proud. Do not let pride keep you from walking in all that God has made available to you. Humble yourself and the Holy Spirit will teach you how to yield and be used in this wonderful gift that He has bestowed upon the church.

Chapter 3
Be Faithful to the Revelation

ॐ

I have learned, when God gives you a revelation or your eyes are opened to a truth, it is important that you be faithful to that revelation. When I first became aware of the prophetic ministry I was in a church where if this was heard of it was never taught or discussed. As a matter of fact, when I began to go where the prophetic was being taught, I was ostracized. My peers began to say things like, "We are telling pastor because you are going to the psychic." So many rude and hurtful comments were made. As I grew in understanding, I began to teach the prophetic. I was called a false prophet and my lifestyle and character were under constant attack by premature judgments or misunderstandings.

Nevertheless, I refused to be diverted because I knew in my heart that prophecy came from God. It was not psychic and I stood strong on my convictions. I was faithful to the revelation that I had received, not because someone gave me a prophetic word, but because I took the revelation of others and studied for myself. I didn't despise or quench the Spirit, but I did do as the Word says. I tried and tested to see if the prophecy was of God.

My first encounter with the prophetic ministry was interesting. I was sitting in a service in the basement of a storefront church and the people were praying in tongues. I thought to myself, "This is strange. What is all of this gibber jabber?" Then the team began to prophesy to certain people in the audience. Making statements like, "I hear the Lord saying," and "the Spirit of the Living God says...". I was so skeptical. I thought to myself, "This is so fake. They're up there saying God said this and that to people and God doesn't even talk to people". So I thought, until they pulled me up. The team members read the very thoughts of my heart even back to a request I had made to God when I was ten years old. As one of the team members prophesied to me I began to cry and I knew it was real.

Now eight years later, after being committed to searching this matter out and studying for myself, God has approved of my diligence and called me to share what I have learned through direct revelation as well as my experiences with this awesome gift from God. I want to encourage you if your church has not embraced the prophetic gifting, do not rebel against the governing authorities. Submit yourself and continue to study to show yourself approved. God will reward your obedience and faithfulness. I'll talk more about this in the chapter on principles, protocol, and procedures of the prophetic gifting.

Prophecy truly is a gift to be valued. When you hear the Words that carry the plans in the mind of God and the feelings that come from His heart and release them into this earthly atmosphere it is phenomenal to partake in the wonders of God's spiritual gifts. One Prophetic Word spoken in 1997 from heaven to me set my life on a course that has generated momentum every since that day.

One Word from God can totally change the course of your life. I have been pressing towards the mark of the High call ever since the first prophetic Word spoken to me. It literally shifted me in a totally different direction. I used to watch the preachers with amazement simply mesmerized by man, but now I know it is not man but the Spirit of the living God within man that causes the manifestations to take place. God wants to use us in the same capacity to impact our home, neighborhood, jobs, regions, country, and other nations. Our pastors can't be everywhere and they can't touch everybody. This is why we must be trained to do the work of the ministry (Ephesians 4:11, 12). We all have a specified sphere of influence. As people of God, we are to think with a panoramic view and not with a tunnel view. Our four and no more will not do. God has big plans and it includes us.

In the midst of casual conversation, the other person may not be aware of it, but because you recognize the Master's voice, God will speak to you through individuals or use you to speak to others. I don't believe the prophetic gifting is one of the gifts we pick and choose. The Spiritual gift of prophecy is a necessity for the Body of Christ. The prophetic ministry is so powerful that I don't think we realize the awesome impact this gift has as it is released to the Body of Christ.

"But he who prophesies speaks to men for their strengthening, encouragement, and comfort" (1 Corinthians 14:3).

God told Ezekiel to Prophesy to the dead and dry bones. There will be times when we will have to suffer and endure during test and trials. The Bible says all those who choose to live Holy must suffer. A word from heaven can put situations and circumstances in proper perspective and you can pick up your cross knowing that there is and expected end (Jeremiah 29:11). As believers we want to know what God thinks about our situation from His perspective. He doesn't want us to be in the dark concerning any aspect of our lives.

"The secret things belong to the Lord our God, but the things revealed belong to us and to our children forever, that we may follow all the words of this law" (Deuteronomy 29:29).

Psychics are not an option, because God has provided the prophetic gifting for the Body of Christ. The police and the people of the world should be coming to us for unrevealed information. God wants to bring home missing children. This is why He gave us the prophetic ministry, so that we may know supernaturally what the natural senses can't detect.

"No eye has seen, no ear has heard, no mind has conceived what God has prepared for those who love Him, but God has revealed it by His Spirit" (1 Corinthians 2:9, 10).

You are an agent of God and He wants to use you to bless His people. There are some things that God wants to reveal to His children personally or by way of the prophetic gifting through the Holy Spirit. When you begin to prophesy you will experience the most miraculous moves of God in the lives of others. When you speak a prophetic Word into what looks like a hopeless situation, you will see the demeanor of individuals change. As the Lord blows the breath of life back into their dead and dry dreams you will have then partaken of the miracles, signs, and wonders of God that the Bible talks about.

The Bible tells us that there is no greater love than to lay your life down (cares and issues) and put another before you to minister to their needs.

"Follow the way of Love and eagerly desire spiritual gifts, especially the gift of prophecy" (1 Corinthians 14:1).

We are encouraged to eagerly desire the gift of prophecy, but most importantly to follow the way of love. Love has got to be the driving force that motivates you to be used in the gift of prophecy. God judges the motive and intent of the heart strictly when the gifts of the Spirit are manifested through you.

"If I have the gift of prophecy and can fathom all mysteries and all knowledge, and if I have a faith that can move mountains, but have not love, I am nothing" (1Corinthians 13:2).

Are Pew Members Approved to Prophesy

Yes! You are approved by God to speak His words. My first prophetic Word stated that I would be a public speaker and a teacher. At that time I thought my great calling was to sing in the choir and come to church faithfully to hear the pastor preach to me. Actually, I did not know I had a calling, nor did anyone tell me. How could God use me to teach others if I didn't know the Word? Therefore, I had to make a decision and I did. I decided that I would study the Bible, not just read it, but search for understanding and comprehension. I began to study by subjects and chapters or books of the Bible. The Lord will meet you wherever you start. If you allow Him to by yielding your will to His, He will get in the driver seat and be your personal pilot throughout your life.

There are some requirements on our part. The Bible says that many are called, but few are chosen. The Lord told me, "Do you know the difference between the called and the chosen?" I said, "No Lord, how do You make this determination?" He responded by saying, "The chosen are the ones that responded to the call." Response is a verb, which means it is marked by action. Therefore, the called became the chosen because of their verbal, as well as physical response. We are all called to do something. God did not create you because He was bored and had nothing else to do. We were all created to fulfill a need in the earth (Romans 8:29, 30).

You have to embrace the truth and mix it with faith. You are a part of God's prophetic army and according to the Bible, faith without works is dead. If you believe this Word, then you will act upon the revelation that you receive. When God introduced the prophetic to my life, I bought tapes and books. I went to seminars, training sessions, and conferences. I invested in my education concerning this gift. I asked and it was given unto me, I sought after the truth concerning the prophetic and I found out no one is exempt; all who want to can be included. I knocked and the Lord opened unto me the door that held the secrets and mysteries of the Kingdom (Matthew 7:7).

I spent money on hotels and conference fees. I traveled to churches locally, as well as out of town. Wherever I heard a church was offering teachings concerning this gifting, I was there. Now what was so miraculous is that the Lord would bring the information right to me. Lansing, Michigan was not moving strongly in this gift, so for a season I had to go where there was prophetic teaching. I followed the Holy Spirit and devoted myself to the teachings and understanding of this gift from God.

"They devoted themselves to the Apostles' teaching and to the fellowship, to the breaking of bread and to prayer" **(Acts 2:42).**

The Apostles were commanded by God and commissioned to go and make disciples. Jesus told them freely you have received and freely you give. Not only did they give the healing power of God to make individuals whole, but also they trained others to do what they were doing. This was the example left by Jesus.

"I tell you the truth, anyone who has faith in me will do what I have been doing, he will do even greater things than these, because I am going to the Father" **(John 14:12).**

The conferences that I attended had Apostles and Prophets that taught us not only from scripture, but we experienced hands-on training. If it was a prophetic conference they held a two-hour session where you actually were trained to open your mouth by faith and speak prophetically. I fell in love with this gift immediately. As someone spoke a prophetic message, I found out that God was concerned about my welfare and He had been keeping tabs on all that the enemy had tried to do to kill, steal, and destroy in my life. God loves us so much and wants to break the design of the enemy off of our lives by sending a message of hope and comfort through prophecy. After receiving my first prophetic Word, my first response was that I must learn how to do that. I yearned for the ability to prophesy, so I could be used by God to bless others as God had so graciously touched me through this gift.

One of the things that Jesus did constantly was prophesy to people. God is calling His children to move into the realm where we begin to do the greater works. This is the reason why He gave us His Spirit. We are supernatural people. We are not just the everyday, average, mediocre, just trying to make it through life type of people. We have the greater One living on the inside of us. We have something to offer the world that they do not have and they need Jesus!

"At this I fell at his feet to worship him. But he said to me, "Do not do it! I am a fellow servant with you and with your brothers who hold to the testimony of Jesus. Worship God! For the testimony of Jesus is the spirit of Prophecy" (Revelation 19:10).

Do you want to be known in the heavens as one who carries the testimony of Jesus? Then prophesy by the Spirit of the living God. The apostle Paul said in **1 Corinthians 2: 4,5, "My message and preaching were not with wise and persuasive words, but with a demonstration of the Spirit's power, so**

that your faith might not rest on men's wisdom, but on God's power". The prophetic ministry is the power of God in operation. There is no way you can know things about people that they have not shared. God knows everything and He reveals it through a prophetic Word sent through a messenger. Remember God's ultimate goal is reconciliation, restoration, edification, exhortation and comfort. It is not to expose people's personal business. We are not to abuse or misuse this gift. It is not for personal gain, to expose, or to bring harm to others.

"But everyone who prophesies speaks to men for their strengthening, encouragement, and comfort" (1 Corinthians 14:3).

The Prophetic Gifting Releases Truth

"But when He, the Spirit of truth, comes, he will guide you into all truth. He will not speak on his own; He will speak only what he hears, and he will tell you what is yet to come" (John 16: 13).

That is what the prophetic ministry is all about. The Holy Spirit revealing unto mankind what the Father tells Him. I encourage you to not allow the devil to rob you of your God-given ability to not only hear His voice for yourself, but also to be a blessing to someone else and relay the messages of God through the prophetic ministry. **"And you shall**

**know the truth and the truth shall set you free"
(John 8:32).**

The spoken Rhema Word of God is the perspective of God and can clear up any delusion and deception that the enemy tries to throw at us. The Holy Spirit is the Spirit of Truth. It is His pleasure to pull the mask off situations and show us what lies beneath. When the enemy comes in like a flood, God will raise up a standard against him. A benefit of the prophetic ministry is that the Spirit of Truth will disclose hidden information to us. When the enemy lies to us and we take the bait, a prophetic Word from God can set the record straight and bring us into the full knowledge and understanding concerning the events that occur in our lives.

The enemy originally has blinded the minds of unbelievers (2 Corinthians 4:4). Sadly, the truth is that some of the believers also go through life with this cloak of darkness in their minds. The prophetic ministry comes to tear down, root out, pluck up, and destroy the works of the enemy so that God can plant the truth in the hearts and minds of His people. Then the church is able to build upon a solid foundation. We were never meant to go to church get goose bumps, go home and struggle through the week until our next meeting session. The church was created to impact the world. If twelve men (the Apostles) could have such a tremendous impact in their day, what is the excuse for the church now? We have more resources, our travel is more advanced, and technology allows us to transfer information at the touch of a finger. Wake up church! It is time to immobilize the prophetic army of God that will go forth and declare the works of the Lord. We must set order and enforce the spiritual laws by decreeing the justice of the Lord. You must prophesy to the elements, people, and your life if you are going to make it in these last days.

As you walk in the truth of the prophetic gifting, you will find that there are different measures of this gift and people walk in different levels and dimensions of the prophetic gifting. **"All these are the work of one and the same Spirit, and he gives them to each one as He determines" (1 Corinthians 12:11).**

It is the Holy Spirit that determines how much and what gifts are distributed throughout the Body of Christ. We all have the ability within us to speak a prophetic message, but not all are called to be a Prophet.

"Are all Apostles? Are all prophets? Are all teachers? Do all work miracles?" (1 Corinthians 12:29).

We all have been given a specific task for the advancing of God's kingdom, and we all have been given a measure of grace and tools to complete our assignments.

"But in fact God has arranged the parts in the body, every one of them just as He wanted them to be. If they were all one part, where would the body be" (1 Corinthians 12:18, 19)?

Our assignments come with a measure of grace and God has equipped us with the necessary tools to fulfill and complete our assignments. Our God made no exclusions; it does not matter what class, color, or size you are. All flesh can prophesy (Acts 2:17,18). **All means exactly that, All!** You can't exist on this earth without being someone's son or daughter, so you are included in this scripture. It is God's desire, it is in His Word, and it is possible for all those that believe. Anything that we do for God, concerning God, and inspired by God must be done by FAITH!

The Bible tells us that whatever a man thinketh in His heart so is he. I think and know that I am a part of God's household. I am a sheep in His pasture and His sheep hear His voice. According to **John 10: 27, "My sheep listen to my voice; I know them, and they follow me".** Therefore, I know I can receive and speak a prophetic message from God. This has got to be your mentality: I may not be a Prophet, but I am a sheep and because I hear His voice I can speak prophetically.

"The watchman opens the gate for Him, and the sheep listen to his voice. He calls his own sheep by name and leads them out. When He has brought out all His own, He goes on ahead of them, and His sheep follow Him because they know His voice" (John 10: 3, 4).

Because you are a sheep, you are on the eligibility and competence list in heaven to be used by

God. God is not like man. He does not lie. If He said you could prophesy because He would give His Spirit without measure in the last days, then the only thing that would lock you out of this prophetic promise is your doubt and unbelief. Doubt and unbelief stifles and stagnates you from moving into the predestined position already prepared for you by God (Romans 8:28, 29). It is not only a part of your destiny to know your God and do great exploits in His name, but you are predestined.

Let's just take a moment and saturate in this awesome revelation. You are called according to His purpose, so quite naturally He wants things done His way with the tools that He has provided. The scriptures say that He foreknew you. In Greek, this word foreknew means chosen before and already known. So, when your destiny was designed, He had you in mind. It is our responsibility to renew our minds so that we are transformed back into our original position and image; which is the likeness of God. If we were designed originally to look like Jesus and act like Jesus, then get ready because the very life of Jesus from Genesis to Revelation is prophetic. **"...Worship God! For the testimony of Jesus is the spirit of prophecy" (Revelation 19:10).** Jesus prophesied to everyone and every living creature and organism that exist (John 1:1-3).

We are already glorified, justified, and called. Our election is made sure before we even discover our purpose in the earth. However, in order to walk in the fullness of our authorized power, we must know who we are and have great faith.

Don't allow fear, doubt, and unbelief to become a fatal attraction in your life. These three enemies, along with skepticism within us, are like magnets. We attract what we believe. These fatal attractions are hard to get rid of once you entertain them. They become a nuisance; they won't take no for an answer. Even if you begin to prophesy they still continue to try and seduce you with their lies. You start to believe that you can only go so far in this gift because you are not a prophet. The enemy questions you asking, "Who qualified you to speak a prophetic message? You have no title or ranking position within the church. You have not been ordained, you can't prophesy as long as Brother Anointed and Appointed. You only have a few words, so you should just sit down when the team goes forth". Lies, lies, lies.

Remember, satan is the father of lies and every thought is to be taken captive and arguments demolished. Don't argue with the enemy. As a matter of fact, don't even allow him the opportunity to speak to your heart- that is God's job. We don't follow the voice of the stranger. We are to guard our hearts with all diligence because the issues of our lives are directly connected to what is stored within our hearts. Because we can have what we say, we shape our world with our words, and therefore the issues we face are a direct result of what we have or have not been confessing.

"I tell you the truth, if anyone says to this mountain, 'Go, throw yourself into the sea, and does not doubt in his heart but

believes that what he says will happen, it will be done for him" (Mark 11:23).

Your heart is affected by what you take in through the gates of the body. There are three main gates that are always in affect. The eye gates, the ear gates, and the information that is downloaded is released through the mouth gate.

Let's first examine the eye gates. **"The eye is the lamp of the body, if your eyes are good, your whole body will be full of light. But if your eyes are bad, your whole body will be full of darkness. If then the light within you is darkness, how great is that darkness" (Matthew 6: 22, 23).** If we are not careful we can become infected as well as affected by the world. What you see, the hype, the portrayal of the supernatural via movies, props, etc, these things taint and distort our perception and understanding of the supernatural. God is the Creator, but the enemy is an imitator. We must be careful what we allow to enter in through our eyes in the natural, because it will and does affect our spirit.

The ear gates are also a key entrance. I figured out when you watch a movie it is the music that builds you up and causes your heart to race as you wait to see with your eyes what will happen next. The impact of a scary movie is no good without good sound effects. *Twilight Zone* had the do-do-do-do. And who could ever forget *Friday the Thirteenth*? You always knew when Jason was about to strike, because you would hear cha-cha-cha-cha-ka–ka-ka-ka. The brain internalizes what we take in through our ear gate. As the command center, the brain sends impulses to the heart and tells it how to react.

If you hear the prophetic promise of your destiny and deny it because of the raindrops of doubt and the winds of unbelief, you will be like the foolish man who builds his house on the sand (Matthew 7:24-27). If your house is not built on the Rock it will not be able to stand.

Your ear gates are a determining factor of what enters your heart because faith is about believing what the natural eye can't see. That is why Christians don't walk by sight; we walk by faith. We are told in the Bible that faith comes by **hearing**. When you hear information enters in through the ear gates and transferred to the brain, but it is only made a reality in your life when it is released into the atmosphere and you take ownership of the Words spoken by you or others.

"The power of life and death is in the tongue and you shall eat the fruit thereof" (Proverbs 18:21). Our words come from our tongue. However, we do not speak from the brain. Our words originate from the heart.

"You brood of vipers, how can you who are evil say anything good? For out of the overflow of the heart the mouth speaks. The good man brings the good things out of the good stored up in Him, and the evil man bring the evil things out of the evil stored up in him" (Matthew 12:34,35).

What is stored in you is what you received through the eye or the ear gates. The received information is filtered through your brain, but like I said before, it only becomes a reality when you speak it. This is why it is important to set a guard at the door of our heart. You can't even receive the gift of salvation unless you hear the good news and make a confession. It can't be one or the other. It must be both the hearing and confessing to make it official.

"The word is near you it is in your MOUTH AND HEART, that is the word of faith WE ARE PROCLAMING: that if you confess with your mouth, "Jesus is Lord," AND believe in your heart that God raised Him from the dead, you will be saved. For it is with your heart that you believe and are justified, AND it is with your mouth that you confess and are saved" (Romans 10:8-10).

We must realize that our thoughts infiltrate our hearts. We must know we are the result of what we speak based upon what we think. We must be careful of our outside influences. AS A MAN THINKETH IN HIS HEART, SO IS HE. That is why we are told to renew our minds and reset our thought patterns. Our thoughts do not come from within ourselves. We are constantly bombarded with thoughts. They are not ours until we take ownership of them. The scripture tells us to be transformed by renewing our mind. To transform means to bring about a change. Changing our minds is equivalent to repenting, which means to turn and go the other way.

God said be transformed so that you will be able to do something. Do not <u>conform</u> to the pattern of this world, but be <u>transformed</u> by the <u>renewing</u> of your mind. Then you will be able to test and approve what God's will is; His good, pleasing and perfect will for your life.

"Do you know for sure it is the will of God for only the prophets to prophesy? What pattern have you fashioned your life after"? (Roman 12:2)

"Beware lest any man spoil you through philosophy and vain deceit, after the tradition of men, after the rudiments of the world, and not after Christ" **(Colossians 2:8).**

"See to it that no one takes you captive through hollow and deceptive philosophy that depends on human tradition and the basic principles of this world rather than on Christ" (NIV)

"Don't let others spoil your faith and joy with their philosophies, their wrong and shallow answers built on men's thoughts and ideas, instead of on what Christ has said" (Living Bible).

We are given a strategy for transformation as we are told to think differently. You can't put new wine in old wineskins. Before new wine can be poured in, the vessel itself must be transformed. A change cannot take place until old thought patterns are made new. If your wineskin is fashioned after the pattern of this world, it won't be able to hold the revelation that all sons and daughters can prophesy.

This is what we speak, not in words taught us by human wisdom but in words taught by the Spirit, expressing spiritual truths in spiritual words. The man without the Spirit does not accept the things that come from the spirit of God, for they are foolishness to him, and he cannot understand them, because they are spiritually discerned" (1 Corinthians 2:13, 14).

These are the last days and God is pouring His Spirit upon all flesh. I admonish you to not miss the outpouring. Be all that you can be in God's army. And remember, **YOU CAN PROPHESY!**

Part II

ೞ

Prophetic Principles, Protocols, and Procedures

"Let all things be done decently and in order"
1 Corinthians 14:40

Chapter 1
PROPHETIC PRINCIPLES

෯෯

We are to keep in mind the principle of operating with decency and in proper order when moving in the gifts of the Spirit (1 Corinthians 14:40 KJV). A principle is known as a comprehensive or fundamental law. It is a rule or code of conduct. There are rules and regulations according to the Word of God that come with this awesome gift. Prophetic principles are boundaries set to keep us from operating in divination and sorcery, as well as bringing us into the knowledge of the code of ethics concerning this gift. The line between prophecy and divination is very thin, but as long as you are submitted to God and the God-given authority set within the Body of Christ, you will stay within the boundary lines. This is God's check-and- balance system that is set as a safety zone for us. It keeps us from being renegades running rampant outside of the covering God has provided for with in the church.

There is a certain reverence and respect that one must carry while walking in the fullness of this gifting. The Lord, unlike man does not look at the anointing and the gifts upon a person's life. God looks at the heart and He sees whom He can trust and with how much He can trust them.

"But the Lord said to Samuel, "Do not consider his appearance or his height, for I have rejected him. The Lord does not look at the things that man looks at. Man looks at the outward appearance, but the Lord looks at the heart" (1 Samuel 16:7).

It is imperative as a Christian that you first allow this gift to be matured and your character developed before you run off and begin to prophesy to the world. Integrity and character is of the utmost importance. What you do when no one is looking is what really counts.

"Slaves, obey your masters with respect and fear, just as you would obey Christ. Obey them not only to win their favor when their eye is on you, but like slaves of Christ, doing the will of God from your heart" (Ephesians 6:5, 6).

You should be submitted to someone who can be a covering for you and an overseer to protect your life. When you submit to leadership established by

God, you avoid pitfalls and traps that are set up to entangle us by the enemy.

"Obey your leaders and submit to their authority. They keep watch over you as men who must give an account. Obey them so that their work will be a joy, not a burden, for that would be of no advantage to you" (Hebrews 13:17).

Our leaders were placed in authority to watch out for us. Sometimes we think that our leaders are trying to hold us back, yet this is not the truth. It may be that you are not ready, or you are being tested by God to see what type of fruit your tree bears. Do you display submission or rebellion when told no? Is there obedience or disobedience growing on your vines when you are told to wait? The gifts and callings of God come without repentance (Romans 11:29). In other words, if you don't repent by turning from ungodly behavior patterns and live holy, you are still called and can move in the gifts of the Spirit. Your leader watches for your soul, but they also were put in your life to help develop your character (1 Samuel 18: 9-11, 19: 18-24). King Saul was full of jealousy, rage, and intended to murder David, but nevertheless he was still called to be King and prophesied while full of ungodly behavior patterns.

Your gifts will bring you before great men, but if you do not get godly character you can be dismissed quickly. Who wants to deal with a gifted individual that won't submit to the ordinances of the house?

Every situation and circumstance that we encounter in life is not always from the devil.

"All scripture is God- breathed and is useful for teaching, rebuking, correcting, and training in righteousness, so that the man of God may be thoroughly equipped for every good work" (2 Timothy 3:16).

God wants us equipped, but at times the methods He uses may not be pleasing to the flesh. Actually, it may be offensive from a carnal point of view, but without a challenge we will not strive for holiness and righteousness.

1. Teaching: to expand and increase one's understanding and knowledge.
2. Rebuking: an act of love to confront an individual that is in an unprofitable state.
3. Correcting: to set what is wrong and make it right.
4. Training in righteousness: to offend the flesh, set the soul under subjection, and teach the Spirit to reign over both.

If for this reason God wrote the scriptures, then quite naturally our leaders are accountable for teaching us through these four elements that we may be thoroughly equipped for the work of the ministry. Don't fight the system designed by God to put your flesh and lustful desires in check. I know personally that the gifts can cause you to get a big head. It is a great feeling to be used by God, but we must stay humble at all times. Pride comes before the fall. That is why leadership has been established and they have a long stickpin that helps deflate all heads that get puffed up. I encourage you to submit to the local leadership in your church. If you do not have a covering, please do not prophesy. It is dangerous to move in spiritual dynamics without a covering (Matthew 7:22, 23).

"Everyone must submit himself to the governing authorities, for there is no authority except that which God has established. The authorities that exist have been established by God" (Romans 13:1).

It was God who established the governmental structure of the church and it is well within reason. I encourage you not to be a renegade. Your very salvation may be put in jeopardy as a result. A renegade is one who deserts their faith or allegiance. These individuals or groups reject lawful behavior. Renegades want to do their own thing and not submit to any rules or regulations. We all must have guidelines because they are set as boundaries to keep us from falling into sin.

Can the gifts get you into trouble? No, but our motives, rebellion, lustful desires, and choices we make without the counsel of the Lord can. Regardless of what drives us, rather it be our motives or wrong intentions, God will bless His people in spite of our inadequacies or insufficiencies. I have seen powerful men and women of God fall hard because they would not allow God to deal with their character flaws. God is committed to our growth and He will expose sinful behavior by pulling the covers off of hidden agendas. Also, full-blown sin will be confronted and revealed. The Apostle Paul refused to be a castaway after ministering to people, for lack of self-control, and discipline of the flesh (1 Corinthians 9: 27).

Our bodies represent the yoking of our flesh to this world. It is inevitable because we have been subjected to this fallen nature, but there is a way of escape. If our flesh wants to rebel, then we should submit. And if we want to talk back, then we should hold our peace. If the spirit of heaviness (depression) tries to come upon us, then it is time to praise. We must beat our bodies into subjection to the ruler-shipping spirits, and then submit to those who are in authority over us.

How can it be that we move in the gifts of the Spirit on earth mightily, but when some of us get to Heaven, the Lord calls some evildoers? The people in the Bible said, "didn't I do these things in your name?" Prophesy, casting out devils, and so forth. God responds by saying yes, but He considers them evildoers. We must remember the gifts and callings upon our lives were given to us before we were put in our mother's wombs (Jeremiah 1:5). Nevertheless, you will still encounter those who will muddy the waters and defile the prophetic rivers within the Body of Christ, because of their lack of submission. God is not mocked. What we sow is what we will reap. The wages of sin is death and it has an insatiable hunger for payment. It must be continually fed in order to survive.

"When a sentence for a crime is not quickly carried out, the hearts of the people are filled with schemes to do wrong. Although a wicked man commits a hundred crimes and still lives a long time, I know that it will go better with God-fearing men, who are reverent before God" (Ecclesiastes 8:11, 12)

Our Works Will be Judged by God

"For no one can lay any foundation other than the one already laid, which is Jesus Christ. If any man builds on this foundation using gold, silver, costly stones, wood, hay or straw, his work will be shown for what it is, because the day will bring it to light. It will be revealed with fire, and the fire will test the quality of each man's work. If what he has built survives, he will receive his reward. If it is burned up, he will suffer loss; he himself will be saved, but only as one escaping through the flames" (1 Corinthians 3:11-15).

God sent a message to Saul through the prophet Samuel. He said obedience is better than any sacrifice you can ever bring forth. With God, the only thing that counts is the Spirit behind our works (1 Corinthians 13:2). Our motives, character, and integrity are forces that release the essential keys that we need to drive all of our efforts for the Kingdom. We will be judged. It is not just what we do for the Lord, but why we do what we do in the name of the Lord that matters. There are many ulterior motives that can be involved when it comes to prophesying. For instance, I used to prophesy so everyone could see how eloquently my words flowed together and how accurate I was in my delivery of a prophetic message. We are encouraged by the Apostle Paul to not be ignorant to the devil's devices. He is always scheming and trying to dilute and pollute the authentic works of God. Pride goes before the fall and that is why the Lord used my leader to say "no" quite a bit to me in the beginning so that my character and integrity could mature along side the gift within me.

Beware and be careful. It is easy to fall into temptation if you are not disciplined. It is easy to embrace the spirit of pride and prophesy for self-exaltation in order to promote your ministry. "Look at me. I am so anointed and I hear the voice of God. Respect me, love me, and follow me." This is a dangerous place to be in, because it is the beginning of idolatry. We should never let others put us up on a pedestal because of our gifts. We are to remind people not to worship us because we are simply messengers. You should always point them back to the Heavenly Father.

"At this I fell at his feet to worship him. But he said to me, "Do not do it! I am a fellow servant with you and with your brothers who hold to the testimony of Jesus. Worship God! For the testimony of Jesus is the spirit of prophecy" **(Revelation 19:10).**

Our lifestyle as prophetic believers is always on display, so it is important to be careful how we live and carry ourselves, before God and before man. Even when we don't realize it, we are being watched, and our fruit is being judged. **"Make a tree good and its fruit will be good, or make a tree bad and its fruit will be bad, for a tree is recognized by its fruit" (Matthew 12: 33).**

How we live our lives everyday is very important. Not just in the church, but outside of the church as well. We have to live a prophetic lifestyle because we are created beings and we are living witnesses of the most High God. Our lives are not only on display in the Kingdom, but also before the lost sheep that watch the church with a magnifying glass.

"Be wise in the way you act towards outsiders; make the most of every opportunity" (Colossians 4:5).

Character and integrity are important parts of the life of a prophetic personality. Principles are God's spiritual laws set in motion, and they apply whether you know about them or not. **"My people perish**

for lack of knowledge" (Hosea 4:6). If a teenager decides that he is going to jump in his parent's car and take it for a spin, and he runs a yield sign, fails to signal when switching lanes, or does not allow the pedestrians the right of way, an officer of the law, who is given the authority to enforce the law, has a legal right to pull the child over and possibly arrest him. Is the child subject to leniency because they did not know the rules and guidelines of the road? No, it is their responsibility to find out the rules of the road are before they drive. They must pay the penalty and suffer the consequences that come with ignorance. Not knowing is not an excuse. The rules have been set for a reason and they will be enforced.

> **"For he is God's servant to do you good. But if you do wrong be afraid, for he does not bear the sword for nothing. He is God's servant, an agent of wrath to bring punishment on the wrong doer. Therefore it is necessary to submit to the authorities, not only because of possible punishmen, but also because of conscience"** **(Romans 13:4, 5).**

This lack of submission is why God said my people perish for lack of knowledge. We have been accepting the wrong information as truth. I used to think, "what I don't know will not hurt me." In fact, what you don't know can be detrimental to your future and a costly set back in fulfilling your purpose in life. Who wants to enter into eternity knowing that they operated in the gifts of the Spirit with powerful moves of God happening while they ministered and yet when they go before the throne, they only hear the Lord say, depart from me you worker of iniquity? Yes, you did prophesy in My name, but did you obey, submit, and follow the instructions according to My Word? God encourages us to get an understanding so that we will not be ruined by ignorance (Proverbs 4:7).

"Everyone must submit himself to the governing authorities, for there is no authority except that which God has established. The authorities that exist have been established by God. Consequently, he who rebels against the authority is rebelling against what God has instituted, and those who do so will bring judgment upon themselves. For rulers hold no terror for those who do right, but for those who do wrong. Do you want to be free from fear of the one who is in authority? Then do what is right and he will commend you" (Romans 13:1-3).

God set up a structure that would keep all of us from self-destruction. I encourage you to adhere to the principle, protocol, and procedures of your local assembly. A wise man once asked a question, "Can you tell me what the back of your head looks like?" I couldn't without a two-way mirror. This is why we need our leaders, because they can see into areas that we overlook. If your hair were sticking out of place in the back of your head you wouldn't know it without someone bringing it to your attention. Sometimes we are in such a rush that when we arrive at our destination someone walks up to us and pulls our collar out of our shirt. I must admit, there have been a few occasions when I have left my house and had a garment on inside out or backwards. We have all been there before and we are not perfect. We can make mistakes and it is okay. There is no mess that we can make that God is not big enough to clean up. Just look at our lives before we were transformed into the Kingdom of God. Nevertheless, when it comes to the lives of people those little unnecessary bloopers can be very costly. Let's take advantage of God's structure and avoid pitfalls. I encourage you to prophesy, but more importantly I encourage you to submit and obey.

I have been driving for some time now and I consider myself a skilled driver. There are still times when I look in the rear view mirror and glance over my shoulder before switching lanes, and yet I still hear a horn blow because I didn't see the car in my blind spot. This is how it is sometimes in the ministry. We can be ever so skilled in the gifts, but there are still times when we have blind spots, which is why I don't mind submitting to leadership. Lone rangers have no one to cover their backs and watch out for them. If your church is not moving in the prophetic gifting, or you are not allowed to prophesy, I encourage you to just sit tight, be still, and know that God is coming your way. He will make a way, but remember we are people of authority, submitted under God-given authority. In addition to the importance of authority, there are several principles that apply when it comes to the prophetic gifting. It would take an entire book to cover all the prophetic principles in the Word of God. Therefore, I'm only going to go over a few.

1. The Importance of Prayer

A consistent prayer life is the number one key to developing your spiritual ears to hear from Heaven. When we pray, we are communicating with the Father. If you want to discern the voice of God, you must spend time talking to Him and allowing Him an opportunity to respond. In order to have a conversation, both parties must be given the opportunity to speak. The next time you pray make sure you stop and listen as God responds.

2. Believe the Prophet and You Shall Prosper

Any time a Word is given, it must be received by faith. **"For we also had the gospel preached to us, just as they did; but the message they heard was of no value to them, because those who heard did not combine it with faith" (Hebrews 4:2)**. When a prophet speaks into your life we are encouraged to believe the Word of the Lord, so we can prosper (2 Chronicles 20:20). There is a reward that is available if you receive God's prophets (Matthew 10:41).

3. Your Response to a Word is Important

When receiving a Word from the Lord, rather it is individual or corporately, you should respond with a shout, clapping, excitement, and most importantly by faith. It doesn't matter if the Word was intended for encouraging, rebuking, or correction. God chastens only those He loves and accepts as sons (Hebrews 12:5,6).

It is a privilege to have the awesome Heavenly Father speak to us directly by prophecy. He loves us and we are to show our appreciation by our response. Mary was given a prophetic Word and her response was key. In Luke 1:28-37, Mary is told she will conceive from the Holy Spirit. She is also told what to name the child, his destiny, and his purpose in the fullness of time. She is even told that she is highly favored and the Lord is with her. This was amazingly great news and I'm sure she also felt anxious, since it was not good to be betrothed and pregnant at the same time. This was not acceptable in those days, but her response is what set heaven and earth into alignment. She agreed with the plan of God and it came to pass just as it was prophesied (Luke 1:38).

I received the same prophetic Word for two years straight. It was given by at least five different people at different times and places about God giving me a house. I didn't cancel the Word, thank God, but I did delay the progress by my own doubt and unbelief. The first Word came in 2000, and it kept coming, but I didn't believe I could have the house. I rejected the Word, so guess what? I didn't receive the prophetic promise, because I was looking through my natural eyes. My focus was on my credit scores, my debts, and my income.

In 2003, I told the Lord if He would send that Word back to me, I would not reject it. I would embrace it and add my faith to it. I received that Word again before the end of 2003. In December of 2004, I was in my first home.

One of the prophets that attended our church during our "Uncorking the Wells" conference asked me during service if I was a homeowner. I replied, "not yet." He further stated, "The Lord said, "Within 90 days you will be a homeowner." I said, "okay," and I went home that evening and began to literally pack up my belongings. I told the Lord that this is my faith in action like Peter stepping out of the boat.

The following day at the prayer breakfast the same prophet came to me and said, "the Lord said that you are believing to small and the three bedroom house that you are looking at is not the one because the house I have for you has six bedrooms and they are going to give it to you for the price that you are asking for." I said, "Okay, praise the Lord."

Of course, the Lord knew that I was looking at three bedroom houses that had the potential for a fourth bedroom possibly in the basement. My husband and I have four children; we needed a four-bedroom home. I had been looking at houses since April of 2004 and it was now November 20, 2004. I called my realtor and told her that I needed her to pull up all of the six bedroom houses in the city. I told her that she was going to think I was crazy, because I had told her not to exceed a certain amount while looking at three and four bedroom houses. This alone was a challenge and now I was asking her to look up six bedroom houses. She found a house that was supposed to be a four-bedroom house exactly one-week from the time the Word was spoken over my life. We looked at the house and there were four bedrooms upstairs and two downstairs. She remembered the prophetic Word and became excited. The bedroom on the first level was listed as a den and the other as an office, which actually made six bedrooms altogether. The price they were asking was $5,000 less than we originally wanted to pay.

Within two weeks of me receiving the prophetic Word, and mixing it with faith, I acted upon the Word. Today my husband and I own the house and did the closing in less than 30 days of the Word being delivered. This was a prophetic promise sent to me by God, but it was delayed because of my doubt and unbelief. How you respond to a Word is very important. This leads us to our next prophetic principle.

4. Prophetic Words Can be Conditional or Unconditional

Some of the Words given in the Bible were based upon the people's response and actions. This is a conditional Word meaning you have a part to play in the Word coming to pass. For instance, if the Lord speaks through an individual and says, "This season is a season of prosperity in the area of finances and health." Yet, you begin to spend, spend, spend, and do not conduct your monetary affairs wisely, then that Word will surely not benefit you. Or perhaps you begin to eat outrageously, refuse to exercise, and lay around never declaring your healing or confessing health and wholeness physically. Then of course, that Word will not benefit you. You must add faith and action to a prophetic Word. On the other hand, there are times that God will send a Word and it is uncon- ditional. This means that God Himself will see to it that the Word comes to pass (Isaiah 45:23).

"When God made his promise to Abraham, since there was no one greater for him to swear by, he swore by himself... "(Hebrews 6:13).

5. <u>A Prophetic Word Can be Spoken to the Past, Present, or Future</u>

Only God knows how quickly a Word will come to pass. A Word was given to Abraham that he would bear a child, but it was God who determined when the Word would come to pass. When the Lord speaks prophetically to future events, it is for hope, inspira- tion, and to reveal His plans. He will bring His people into awareness in advance, of an expected end that He has prepared from His perspective (Jeremiah 29:10- 14). Regardless of what we see, with an expected end in view based on a prophetic Word from the Lord, we can hold on to hope. Faith is the substance of things hoped for and a timely prophetic Word will mani- fest the evidence of the things we could not see from our viewpoint. Joel spoke of the last days (the future) when God would pour out His Spirit upon all flesh and sons and daughters would prophesy. However, this prophetic Word did not come to pass until we reached the book of Acts (Acts 2:17, 18).

Jesus prophesied to the woman at the well and told her of her past relationships as well as her present condition (John 4:16-18). When the Lord speaks to the present situation it may be for comfort or to let you know that He is aware of your present circumstance. Sometimes He even reassures us in the midst of trials that He has not left us. If the Lord sends a Word concerning the past, most of the time it is to bring healing, restoration, as well as reconciliation in certain areas of our lives. There are so many examples of prophetic Words spoken throughout the Bible to the past, present, or future. Enjoy your study time as the Holy Spirit brings illumination in this area.

6. <u>When a corporate or Individual Word Goes Forth, Anyone Can Benefit From the Word Spoken, If They Receive It With Faith.</u>

"You will say then, branches were broken off so that I can be grafted in, Granted; but they were broken off because of unbelief, and you stand by faith. Do not be arrogant, but be afraid" (Romans 11:19, 20).

A Promise was made to the people of God, but because of unbelief they did not receive the promise.

Yet, the Gentiles were able to walk in the blessing and promises because of their faith. The prophetic promise was spoken and did not return to God void. The Word sent accomplishes what it was sent to do, even if someone else reaps the benefits.

When a prophetic promise is spoken, it will not return to God void. God said His words are Spirit and they are life, so therefore, when they are breathed into our atmosphere it can be applied and benefited by whoever embraces it. If you are in a service and the Word comes forth and you feel like that Word pertains to you, grab it and put it in your pocket. Then mix it with faith and believe God for its manifestation.

If there is a full congregation and only a few individuals receive prophetic Words, you don't have to feel left out. God knows exactly where you are sitting. We as individuals are vessels and we are limited from a physical standpoint. God on the other hand, is omnipotent (all powerful), and He is not limited. He is omniscient (all knowing); He knew you would be present to hear the Word. He is omni-present (everywhere at once). While the minister is releasing Words prophetically, God is right next to you showering you with His love. God's Words are full of life and power and beneficial for all. I have sat in many services where a prophetic Word has gone forth over someone and I can identify with the Word. I received the Word as if I was the one standing up there. God is not a respecter of persons. We have to upgrade and learn to embrace spiritual acts form a spiritual perspective (1 Corinthians 2:12-14).

7. Long Prophetic Words Does Not Mean They are Better or Ensure Accuracy

The proof is in the manifestation. **"But the prophet who prophesies peace will be recognized as one truly sent by the Lord only if his prediction comes true" (Jeremiah 28:9).** It is not the length that makes a prophetic Word or the deliverer of the Word (powerful and anointed). We are moved easily by what we see. One Word from God can save, change, and redirect the order of steps in a person's life. When a Word is delivered we should judge the quality, not the quantity of what has been spoken.

8. Just Because a Prophet's Words Do Not Come to Pass, it Does Not Make Him a False Prophet

"If what a prophet proclaims in the name of the Lord does not take place or come true, that is a message the Lord has not spoken. That prophet has spoken presumptuously. Do not be afraid of him" (Deuteronomy 18:22).

It is possible to get ahead of God or even move with too much zeal. We must also remember not to stone the messenger when speaking prophetically to the future. Sometimes it may take time for the Word to come to fruition. We have to wait on God's timing. Also, something within those receiving the Word may need to come into alignment before the

Word can be made manifested in their lives. This is why God is raising up people who can bring clarity through teaching and books to train His people so we can be thoroughly equipped and avoid pitfalls in this area.

9. <u>Women Can be Prophets and Woman Are Called to Release Prophetic Words</u>

The Bible makes mention of many Prophetess. Women are called to speak for the Lord as well as men (Exodus15: 20; Judges 4:4; 2 kings 22:14; Nehemiah 6:14; Isaiah 8:3; Luke 2:36). The evangelist Phillip in Acts 21:8, 9, had four daughters who also prophesied. If you are born into this world and you are a female, then you also qualify because the prophetic daughters of destiny shall prophesy (Acts 2:17, 18)!

10. <u>Do Not Harm God's Prophets</u>

Prophets are God's servants whether they are right or wrong, live holy, or have character flaws. God chooses who He wants to use, and that is His business. God gives specific instructions in the book of Psalms; **"Do not touch my anointed ones; do my prophets no harm" (Psalms 105:15).** You can interpret that any way you want to, but I choose to be safe and not harm in word or deed God's prophets. Jesus says the forefathers actually physically killed the prophets, but He holds the generation that rejects the prophets accountable as well (Luke 11:47-51).

They only participated mentally and verbally, but they share in the penalty. You may not physically kill God's prophets, but we know that the power of life and death is in our tongues and that verse tells us that we shall eat the fruit of our words. This is a prophetic principle that deserves acute attention.

11. <u>Prophets and Prophetic People Will Suffer Persecution, and Rejection if They Are Authentic</u>

All who want to live holy must suffer persecution. Don't get your feathers all ruffled because it is common and scriptural to be rejected. Not everyone embraces the prophetic gifting. The Apostle Paul said it was his desire to become all things to all men that he may win souls into the Kingdom. For those who will receive, give them all that the Lord will allow you to. For those who won't, don't throw your pearls before swine.

Everyone is not going to honor this awesome gift. A wise woman of God told me something that has helped me sustain my sanity. I believed everyone was supposed to like me and accept me as a friend, so when I was rejected in ministry I was devastated. She said, "Everyone is not called to you in ministry." For those who are not called to you, God will have someone else to minister to them. Look at it from this perspective; there are thirty-one flavors of ice cream at Baskin and Robbins. If you don't like vanilla, rocky road, or butter pecan, there is still chocolate, strawberry and an entire assortment of flavorful varieties from which you can choose. God knows your flavor and He has someone that can meet the needs of everyone in the diversified culture in which we live.

12. Prophets and Prophetic People Can Get Off as Two Left Shoes

It is important that in order to look spiritual, you don't become spooky and flaky. You should never manufacture a prophetic Word. If you don't hear anything, then I warn you not to make something up. Prophetic people can prophesy with wrong motives and move out prematurely, as well as presumptuously. The key is to be led by God or wait upon the Lord. If you are not sure, keep you mouth closed and wait for confirmation and clarification (Isaiah 9:15; Jeremiah 6:13; 14:13, 14; 23:10, 11, 14, 16; Lamentations 2:14).

The Word does not say they are false prophets, but for whatever reason they are not in alignment with the will of God. In one scripture God says He did not send them, then in another he states, **"If they had sat in my council they could have proclaimed My Words" (Jeremiah 23:18, 22).** The Lord's chosen vessels can get off track, as did the prophets of God, who were created to be mouthpieces for the Lord. Likewise, if our motives and lifestyle is anything else than holy we too can get off track.

Some move prematurely and try to promote their ministry. The wise thing to do is wait on the

Lord. You do not need to make room for your gift. The Lord opens doors for you and your gift makes room for you. Have you ever seen a pushy person make room for themselves in a crowded room? The Word says, when you enter a room sit towards the back. There may be someone of greater honor than you present. Don't come to the front or else you will be humiliated when you are asked to move (Luke 14:8-11). Also, if you are invited to come to the front, you will be honored, when the Lord is ready. Stay humble and God will do the moving in His time.

I have been a witness to the downfall and demise of many in the Body of Christ as a result of these forceful actions. There is grace and mercy, even forgiveness for all. However, the effects of the actions of those who move prematurely, but not according to knowledge, can leave lasting scars on people as well as a reproach on themselves. Wait on God and allow Him to promote you so you can walk in integrity and character in the ministry.

"I did not send these prophets, yet they have run with their message; I did not speak to them, yet they have prophesied. But if they had stood in my council, they would have proclaimed my words to my people and would have turned them from their evil ways and from their evil deeds" **(Jeremiah 23:21, 22).**

13. There were False Prophets in the Biblical Days and They Still Exist Today

These are not the same as prophets who prophesy falsely. How do you recognize a false prophet? False prophets do not work for God; they work for the enemy (John 10:12, 13). They pretend to care about the sheep and the plans of God, but they are really interested in their own selfish gain (Mark 13:22; Matthew 7:15, 24:11; Luke 6:26; 2 Peter 2:1; Revelation 16:13, 14, 19:20). They have a form of godliness, but they deny the power thereof. When we prophesy, love should be the driving force; our only source of power comes from God, who is love (1 Corinthians 13:1-3). False prophets are not driven by love, but they are driven by their lust for power and control (Acts 8:4-23; 13:6-10).

14. There Are Many Ways that God Speaks to Us

"For God does speak- now one way, now another- though man may not perceive it. In a dream, in a vision of the night, when deep sleep falls on men as they slumber in their beds, he may speak in their ears and terrify them with warnings" (Job 33: 15-16).

All messages are not received or given in verbal communicating words alone. We serve a very unique and creative God. He speaks verbally, but He also sends messages through images, pictures, visions, dreams, and trances (Numbers 12:6; 1 Samuel 9:9; Ezekiel 40:2; Daniel 1:17; Zechariah 1:8; Luke 1:22; Acts 9:10-12). The Lord also uses demonstrations as a way of communicating (Exodus 7:10-12; 2 Kings 13: 14-21; Jeremiah 13:1-7; 32:6-15; Ezekiel 4:1-5; 37:1-10; Hosea 1:2). These are only a few scriptures that show us how God expresses Himself that transcends verbal communication. Have fun journeying through the Bible to see how He used ordinary people in extraordinary ways to communicate His will in the earth through the different prophetic dimensions.

15. A Prophetic Word Will Keep

If you receive a message from heaven, you don't have to give the Word at that time. You must adhere to the protocol of your local assembly out of respect before you stand up and begin to prophesy. If this is the order of the house, then by all means flow with the Holy Spirit. If it is not acceptable to just stand and prophesy whenever you feel led (we must be Spirit led) then don't disrespect or disrupt the service without permission from leadership.

Most local assemblies have prophetic teams established and set in place. These prophets have been trained, their character has been developed, and they have been released to prophesy over the church. You may have a genuine Word from God, but rebellion or disorder is not God's way of doing things.

"Wherefore, brethren, covet to prophesy, and forbid not to speak in tongues. Let all things be done decently and in order" (1 Corinthians 14: 39, 40 KJ).

What should you do if you have a Word and your leadership does not allow you to speak? Keep silent! You and you alone control the use of your mouth. The spirits of prophets are subject to the control of prophets (1 Corinthians 14:32). God won't force you to speak out of order. Also, He created us with free will, and satan can't force you to be disorderly. He can only plant a seed or entice you with bait. You are your greatest influence. Ultimately, any action that you take is your decision. You determine which voice you will follow.

If God gives you a Word, don't worry. He either gives you a window of opportunity to speak or He will move you to a place where you will be appreciated as a gift to the Body of Christ, not just tolerated. Everything that God tells you or shows you is not to be released verbally. Sometimes, the knowledge is given to you so you can pray and intercede. All of the secrets and revealed things are not to be spoken. Can God trust you with the secrets of the Kingdom (2 Corinthians 12: 3, 4)?

16. <u>Beginners Should Not Correct or Rebuke Until Seasoned or Released by Leadership</u>

You almost can't go wrong encouraging, uplifting, and comforting if you stick within what I call the safety zone. Everyone who prophesies speaks to men for their edification, exhortation, and comfort (1 Corinthians 14:3 KJV). As a novice, there is little to no room for error if you stay within these boundary lines. The prophetic Word spoken into the atmosphere carries a tremendous amount of power and should not be taken lightly.

Ezekiel prophesied to the dead and dry bones and the vast army lived once again. God spoke the world into existence and by His powerful Word everything is created and sustained (Hebrews 1:3). How much more should we take heed and understand that the words we speak contain the power of life and death, especially when heaven is backing them up? When dealing with the lives of people, there is little room for error. If you are just learning how to operate within the prophetic gifting then edification, exhortation, and comfort is the safest way to prophesy.

17. <u>You Must Have Faith to Operate in the Prophetic Gifting</u>

Faith is an essential key to operating in the prophetic anointing. We have different gifts, according to the grace given us. If a man's gift is prophesying, let him use it in proportion to his faith (Romans 12:6). We are told to find out what pleases God (Ephesians 5:10.) Yet, the Bible tells us that without faith it is impossible to please the Lord (Hebrews 11:6).

God's desire is to relate and communicate with His people. Faith comes by hearing the Word of God, so you must continuously read the Word, hear the Word, and cultivate the planted seed of the Word within you, so that your faith can continue to grow. You can do anything through Christ, who gives you strength. Jesus is the Living Word (John 1:1). The Spirit of prophecy is the testimony of Jesus (Revelations 19:10). The scriptures testify of His goodness. If you want to prophesy, then you must know the Lord's language, which is the written Word of God. As you feed your spirit with the Word, your faith will be developed and begin to increase and then you can prophesy according to your faith. On a scale of 1-10, God may have granted you a level 7 for the measure of grace to operate in the prophetic gifting. If your faith is at level 3, then you will not take advantage of the full measure that has been allotted to you (1 Corinthians 12:11). The prophetic is not based on human wisdom and knowledge. It is accomplished according to your faith and obedience.

18. The Prophetic Gift was Given to the Body of Christ to Serve Others Not Yourself

We are not to take advantage of this gift and use it for our own benefits. We are to serve others.

"Each one should use whatever gift he has received to serve others, faithfully administering God's grace in it's various forms. If anyone speaks, he should do it

**as one speaking the very words of God.
If anyone serves, he should do it with the
strength God provides, so that in all things
God may be praised through Jesus Christ.
To him be the glory and power forever and
ever. Amen" (1 Peter 4:10, 11).**

Also, we are not to prostitute this gift. What do
I mean when I say prostitute the gift? I am talking
about making money by selling prophesies, or
charging outrageous fees using this gift in the name
of being a blessing to God's people. Jesus said freely
you have received, so freely you should give. What
has been given to you has come from above and it is
rewarding when you align yourself with the principles and procedures in the Bible concerning this gift.
It is true the Bible tells us that a worker is worth his
keep, but when it comes to being a blessing, the Word
reminds us that if we give it shall be given unto us. If
you charge money in exchange for a prophetic Word,
you are no different than a psychic. It is also important that you don't allow anyone to prostitute you by
drawing a large crowd so they can make money off
you as a gift to the Body of Christ. It is imperative
that we as children of God keep everything that we
do in proper perspective.

19. Prophetic Words Must be Tested

Just because someone speaks a Word in the
name of the Lord does not mean it comes solely
from God. We learned that people could prophesy

presumptuously or out of their own imaginations. We also have to remember that a Word from heaven is spoken to our spirit, filtered through our minds where our words are calculated to form sentences, and then released through our mouths with our attitude and our personality attached to it. Moses was told to speak to the rock and he hit it out of anger (Numbers 20:8). We are still held accountable for every word that we speak in the natural or prophetically (Matthew 12:37). Be careful that you deliver God's Word correctly and remember He said He draws others with loving-kindness.

It is good and scriptural to try the spirit and the prophecy by the Word of God. **"Dear friends, do not believe every spirit, but test the spirits to see whether they are from God" (1 John 4:1).** Test the prophecy to see if it lines up with the way God does things. Is it in accordance to the will of God for your life? The Lord said He wants to give you peace, prosper you, and bring you to an expected end (Jeremiah 29:11 KJ). If you receive a Word of correction, rebuke, or warning, there is a way of escape (1 Corinthians 10:13). We prophesy in part and the messenger has free will in the delivery of the Word. God releases a portion of His will for your life in a prophetic Word. In other words, if you receive a prophetic Word it is not necessarily the totality of God's will for your life. **"For we know in part and we prophesy in part" (1Corinthians 13: 9).** After receiving a prophetic Word, you should go home and get before the Father. Ask Him to bring further revelation to your spirit. It is written,

"No eye has seen, no ear has heard, no mind has conceived what God has prepared for those who love him"- but God has revealed it to us by his spirit (1 Corinthians 2:9, 10). There are times when you will have to get the rest of the story from the secret place. Jesus is the author and finisher of our faith (Hebrews 12:2). He wrote our story. Why then do we want to ask everyone else when we have the ability to go to the One who created us? Jesus knows everything about you and He will speak to you, if you will listen. Remember the messenger only knows the part that God reveals.

20. <u>When Ministering Prophetically You Should Not Strip People of Their Dignity</u>

If a prophetic Word of a personal nature is being given and it is in a public setting, you should lower the microphone and speak directly into the person's ear to ensure their dignity. People have been beaten up, abused, misused, and humiliated enough by life itself, both within the church, as well as outside of the church. Remember our ministry is reconciliation and restoration. We are not called to humiliation, which causes separation (2 Corinthians 5:18, 19). It is not God's will or desire to humiliate His children. The Lord may warn a person in an attempt to get their attention. He will release a Word of correction or rebuke, but it is never His intention to tear His children down. His very desire is to draw all men unto Himself.

The Lord told me to deliver a prophetic Word once to a friend. I thought the Word was very harsh. He said, "Tell her if she does not quit sinning, she is going to die." I waited until the end of service and I chose my words very carefully. I told her, "Remember Lot's wife!" The very next day she called me. She told me that while she was preparing for work she planned to watch television. As soon as she turned the television on, Joyce Meyers said, "Remember Lot's wife!" Although I did not know it, she had been involved in sinful acts. However, God knows every-thing. He sent a Word of warning and she fell out of the church for a season. She was a very faithful and active member of the church, but she did not heed the warning. Thankfully, she's back now and serving the Lord once again- hallelujah!

The point is, the Lord gave me a message and I chose the delivery. I could have been nasty or acted like I was so holy and made her feel guilty and shameful because of what God had revealed to me concerning her. Instead, I chose to use a loving approach so she would receive the Word from God and not reject it because of my attitude or person-ality getting in the way of God's work. We must be wise in our delivery. I don't encourage you to change the message God gives you. Nevertheless, seasoned saints that operate in this gift should know how to deliver a prophetic Word when it comes to warning, correction, and rebuke. As God usually does, He confirmed the Word. He is not obligated to back up what He did not say.

21. <u>Teamwork is Essential in the Last Days</u>

"Submit to one another out of reverence for Christ" (Ephesians 5:21).

One essence of success is to know those who labor among you. We also have to be willing to yield to one another. God has not called us to be lone rangers. Jesus sent them out two by two. In the Old Testament, the prophets spent most of their journey alone, but they still had apprentices that they mentored. One person does not have it all and cannot do it all. Even Jesus brought twelve close to Him to impart into for the work of the ministry. God has arranged the Body in such a way that we cannot help but need each other (1 Corinthians 12:18-21).

According to the Apostle Paul, it takes two people and God himself to help a planted seed grow. That same principle applies today. I planted the seed, Apollos watered it, but God made it grow (1 Corinthians 3:6). I have seen the dynamics of more than one person ministering to a congregation as well as individual prophecies. It is phenomenal. The Lord Jesus Christ Himself distributed grace among the members of the Body of Christ, and said it would take all five of the ministry gifts that He gave unto man to perfect the saints (Eph. 4:11-13). If all five are not in operation in your local assembly then your members will be lopsided, lacking, and not well rounded as they are prepared for the work of the ministry.

If Jesus knew it would take team effort to get the job done, then we should also embrace the revelation.

We prophesy in part, so it's going to take your part as well as my part to effectively get the job done (1 Corinthians 13:9). We are to yield to the Lord as a team player in all that we do. Our God is an advocate of team ministry (1 Corinthians 12:12, 27).

22. The Prophetic Gifting is Key and Strategic in the Operation of the Other Gifts

There are nine gifts listed in 1 Corinthians 12:8-10. They are the Word of knowledge, Word of wisdom, faith, healing, miraculous powers, prophecy, discerning of spirits, tongues, and interpretation of tongues. Prophecy, in its simplest form, is hearing the voice of God and speaking a message concerning what you hear. All prophetic Words have the elements of a Word of knowledge, which is obtaining information supernaturally, not from an earthly descent (Matthew 16:15-17, 9:4; Acts 5:1-4). A prophetic Word could also contain a Word of wisdom, which is the supernatural ability to know what to do in any given situation. This is not the wisdom of man, which is based on life's experiences, trial, and error. This is the wisdom of God supernaturally intervening to bring you to an expected end (2 Kings 5:10; 1 Chronicles 12:32; Jeremiah 29:11).

The Lord not only wants us to work together as a team, but when moving in the gifts of the Spirit you will find that the gifts also team up to accomplish the task at hand. How can you discern a spirit unless through a Word of knowledge God reveals what is present? If you are led by God to lay hands on someone for healing or move miraculously in signs and wonders, you need the Holy Spirit through a Word of knowledge to tell you which way He wants to manifest Himself. For almost all of the gifts of the Spirit you need to hear the voice of God. The prophetic gifting is exciting and a very necessary tool given to us for this end time generation. Woe to the generation that will allow the psychics to outdo the church. We are to rule and have dominion in the earth.

Don't be left behind drinking old wine. Change your wineskin so that you may be able to hold the new wine for this century. God is grooming a prophetic army of believers. Will you be willing to enlist and allow the Holy Spirit to train you in the art of speaking prophetically? All flesh can prophesy!

Chapter 2
CHURCH PROTOCOL
CONCERNING THE PROPHETIC

ॐ

"Wherefore brethren, covet to prophesy,
and forbid not to speak with tongues. Let
all things be done decently and in order"
(1 Corinthians 14:39, 40 KJ).

According to Webster's dictionary, protocol is defined as a code prescribing strict adherence to correct etiquette and procedure. It is a specific way of doing things or a detailed plan of "how to." Protocol is a set of basic guidelines for obeying rules and regulations. There must be structure in the house of God or else we will become like those in the Old Testament in which everyone did what they thought was right in their own eyes (Judges 21:25 KJ). There is an order set in the church and ordained by God. We are to submit our gifts and talents first of all to the Lord, then to the ruling authorities appointed by God.

"Submit yourselves for the Lord's sake to every authority instituted among men: whether to the King, as the supreme authority, or to the governors, who are sent by Him to punish those who do wrong and to commend those who do right" (1 Peter 2:13-15).

The order of each local assembly differs by region, denomination, and leadership. It is important that you know the protocol of your local assembly before you go forth in the spiritual gifts. If you know the ordinances of the church you attend and adhere to them, it will save you from a lot of heartache and grief. If the house that God placed you in does not have a prophetic flow, nor allow the gifts to come forth, then you should submit your gifts to the house. This way you do not give the enemy a foothold and allow disobedience and rebellion to enter into your temple. Until the leader releases you, or they come into the full knowledge of the gifts of the Spirit, it is wise to submit yourself to the governing authorities. A student is not above his teacher. If you do your own thing without permission it is considered rebellion in the eyes of the Lord. Your prophetic rivers will still flow, but they will be muddy and contaminated.

I have been in a situation where God planted me in a house for a season and I knew I was called to train individuals to learn how to operate together on prophetic teams. However, we could only go so far in this gifting. The leader shut down the prophetic classes three times within two years for various reasons (religious protestors, traditional descendants murmuring and complaining). If I would have gone off and did my own thing I would not be where I am today. I would have to walk out the test of submission and obedience again and again until the Lord saw the results that He desired. Obedience and submission are top priority within the lifestyle of a prophetic believer. If you can't obey the ordinances of man, how can you obey the Spirit of the Lord when He says speak or do not speak?

I would have sacrificed promotion and precious time by having to repeat the test of obedience. The Lord once told me, "I'm working out of you some things so that I may put My ways in you through situations that you encounter." With that knowledge the real question is, how will you respond when things don't go the way you think they should?

God is more concerned about our character rather than our abilities. I have come to find every thing that does not go my way in the church is not an attack from the devil. It may very well be the Lord's hand upon you, allowing situations to transform you from the pattern of this world into His image and likeness in all areas of your life. I have made up in my mind that I am determined to pass every test that comes my way. Whether it is initiated by God or the enemy, I am determined not to repeat any test and waste precious time.

"Now it is required that those who have been given a trust must prove yourself faithful" (1 Corinthians 4:2). You prove yourself faithful by your actions and reactions. Actions show what has dominion over you, because what is inside of you (faith, obedience, submission, rebellion, anger, rage) will be displayed when situations occur. These things may lurk in the shadows of your heart, but they are undeniable and when aroused they will manifest and perform.

Between the beginning of my walk with the Lord and today there has been a "Yes, Lord" released in my Spirit. Even in times when I don't agree, I have learned to hush, submit, and obey. Those three acts have brought me through levels of promotion supernaturally that would have taken the average believer many years to accomplish. We are all in training and our sessions never stop, they just increase in intensity as we go from glory to glory and level upon level. You can ask any general serving right now in the army of God. They may be on a higher level and made it through boot camp, but I guarantee you they are still being tried by God.

The Lord once told me that we would have quizzes and tests, but it does not stop there. For some professions, you must take a test to renew your license because of new medications and laws that are being set in place as an alternative or to replace the existing license. If you are a driver, every couple of years you must take a test to renew your drivers' license. In the Kingdom, we can and should advance.

We must be continually upgrading. As we work out our soul salvation we will encounter tests.

Tests are given:

1. To prove our commitment to the Lord and His ordinances.
2. To prove to the enemy who we belong to and where our faith lies.
3. To see where God has brought us from and to bring change in our attitudes and behavior patterns.

If you are not allowed to operate in the gift of prophecy because your leader forbids it, or you have been sat down for any reason, just obey.

"If a ruler's anger rises against you, do not leave your post; calmness can lay great errors to rest" (Ecclesiastes 10:4).

Maybe the gift of prophecy has not been accepted in your church yet. Do not fret. God is restoring this gift back into the Body of Christ and He knows where your local assembly is located. You don't want to open yourself up to a spirit of mutiny, which is subtle, but deadly. You can fall prey by whispering, complaining, and gathering people to yourself that agree with you. Mutiny is when a crew of people follows behind an unauthorized self-made leader to overthrow the set leader. There is such a fine line between rebellion and witchcraft. This is dangerous and you don't want to play this close to the fence.

The spirit of deception and the spirit of mutiny work together, hand-in-hand. The clever thing about these two spirits is that most people who fall prey don't even know they are being deceived and used by the enemy to divide. The very nature of the spirit of deception's character and sole purpose is to stay undetected so it can continue to work through a vessel. The sad thing is if you are not submitted under someone ordained by God to detect the enemy and bring correction in love, then you may find out a little too late that you were in error. The astronomical results of sin can reverberate through time and cause great devastation. Thank God for grace and mercy, but the laws and principles of God still stand and He will not be mocked. Whatever you sow while you are serving in another man's vineyard is what you will attract. You can reap rebellion, mutiny, disobedience, or love, faithfulness, obedience, and submission. The choice is up to you. It is a terrible thing to fall into the hands of the Lord. I want to encourage you to get it straight now. We can all prophesy, but we must submit to the leadership of our local assembly (Hebrews 10: 26, 27, 31).

God will be your advocate when you do what is right, because He is a vindicator. It is in the midst of trials that He educates and prepares us for the work of the ministry. I encourage you not to rebel, but to embrace every situation as a learning experience. Remember your gifts will make room for you, not you make room for your gifts. If you have to sit on your gifts for a season, don't just be a bump on a log and do nothing. Increase your understanding by studying to show yourself approved in this area. While in your time of waiting patiently, the Word says that our name is written in the palm of God's hand so know that you are on His mind. In due time, your gifts will bring you before great men.

Whatever you do, wait on God and do not step outside of the boundary lines of proper protocol and contaminate your prophetic rivers. If you are not able to go forth it may be your character God is developing so you won't be lopsided like a seesaw. You may be awesome in the gifts of the Spirit, but if your disposition is nasty, mean, and uninviting this is not a display of the attributes of our Heavenly Father. God said with loving-kindness He draws us. If there is no love, compassion, or kindness within your prophetic flow, let God work on you. Maybe your fruit is not ripe enough for others to eat.

We don't want to exclude the fact that your leader may just be an unjust ruler. It happened to King David when he was serving King Saul. The Bible said he kept a jealous eye on him and spent most of his time trying to kill him. Whatever the reason, what the enemy means for bad, God turns it around and uses it towards our good. Our Lord wants us to be well proportioned and balanced in every aspect of our Christian walk. So be of good cheer and wait upon the Lord.

If you are released to prophesy, I encourage you not to do it behind closed doors. Let your Words be given in the open so they can be weighed and judged by those who are set to protect and watch over the house of God (Hebrews 13:17). Personal prophecy should be judged, especially if you are not seasoned in this gifting (1 Corinthians 14:29). This protects you and the receivers because we prophesy in part (1 Corinthians 13:9).

"The spirits of prophets are subject to the control of prophets. For God is not a God of disorder but of peace" (1 Corinthians 14:32, 33).

Many lives have been displaced because of a prophetic Word given and the person responds outside of the timing of God. Jesus made a public spectacle of His enemies. He did not hide behind closed doors and neither should we. Allow your prophetic Words to be judged for your safety and the safety of others. Otherwise, you are no different from the psychics luring people into dark shadows to read them their future or control their lives in the name of prophecy.

Say for instance, an individual receives a prophetic Word saying that they are called to be a pastor and they just got saved last week. Do you think it is time for them to pastor a flock of sheep? No sir, they have just begun the process of salvation. The Bible speaks of a novice not being put into an office right away (1Timothy 3:6). Or consider Sister Sally Sue. She received a Word that she is going to the nations. Therefore, based upon the Word she buys a ticket, leaves her children, husband, and job, as she flies on the friendly skies to Jamaica. She knows nothing about spiritual warfare and ruling principalities. She has no prayer covering, because she is not submitted to a local church where the shepherd can watch for her soul and have the intercessors praying for her. Worst of all, God is not backing her because she is acting outside of His timing.

We prophesy in part and most times when a Word of knowledge is given a Word of wisdom may not accompany it. If there are not detailed instructions accompanying a prophetic Word, then you must know that there is always a process to be walked out before you see the fruition of the Word come to pass. Zeal, but not according to knowledge, can get you sidetracked, derailed, and even result in sickness, illness, (physical, emotional, mental) or a premature death. Our enemy does not want prisoners of war; he wants us out of the way. If you do anything outside of the spiritual covering the Lord has provided, you are headed for trouble. Can God redeem us? Yes, but why go through the heartache and pain if the pitfalls can be avoided simply by following proper protocol?

Let's take one more scenario into account. Brother "Just Got Saved," receives a Word that he is a mighty Intercessor. He then begins to come to intercessory prayer with all of his grandiose ideas and tries to implement them without submitting to the leader of intercessory prayer. He has to be corrected in love because he didn't understand the process that takes place from the time you receive a Word to its manifestation. He rebels and then starts to whisper in the other Intercessors' ears. Soon he is like David's son Absolom and has started mutiny against the appointed leader. We know the Bible says that a house divided against its self cannot stand. However, because a saint has opened the door, the enemy has been given access into this local assembly. All Words should be judged.

We prophesy in part. Without fully understanding the missing element that is not always attached to a prophetic Word, the process that lies in between the Word being given and the manifestation of it coming to pass must be taken into account. You are not limited to giving a prophetic Word inside of the church only, unless this is your church's protocol. If you have been given the liberty to prophesy outside of your local assembly make sure it is Spirit-led or you will be like the prophets who prophesied presumptuously or out of their imaginations. If you are on the receiving end of a Word given outside of your local assembly, then you should take that Word to your leader so it can be properly judged. There is safety in the multitude of counselors.

Usually in a setting where prophetic Words are given, they are given in part. A prophetic Word is just that, a prophetic Word. In the midst of a service, the majority of the time you don't have time for questions, teaching, and counseling concerning a prophetic Word. You speak what you hear or see. Jesus is the only One that knows the whole story. When you receive a prophetic Word, it is good to get with the Author and Finisher of your faith and allow God to expound or counsel you pertaining to the information given in a prophetic Word. We are told to try the Spirit by the Spirit, not by flesh and blood. Also, it is important as the giver of the Word that you do not get into the habit of allowing people to try to get you to explain a prophetic Word. We prophesy in part and as a caution it is best that you do not fall into error. The Holy Spirit will bring them into all truth as that is His job (1 Corinthians 2:11, 12).

When prophesying on a team, make sure you are considerate of your fellow team members. Allow them an opportunity to participate in the movement of the Holy Spirit. Be mindful of the time, the flow of the service, and it is important to take into account the amount of people receiving ministry when ministering in a corporate setting. It is not wise to give a thirty-minute prophecy if you have two or three other teammates waiting to go forth. Show some common courtesy and allow your fellow teammates to be used by God. Also, assess the crowd. You don't want to lose the people and cause the Spirit of the God to become quenched. This is not always the case, but these are nuggets to consider when moving with the Holy Spirit in the gift of prophecy.

In a corporate setting only one person should go forth at a time. Allow others to speak and be used by God if you are a part of a team. Also, if a revelation comes to someone who is sitting down, the first speaker should stop. **"For you can all prophesy in turn so that everyone may be instructed and encouraged" (1 Corinthians 14:30, 31).**

Once a prophetic Word has been sealed, you should not come behind the leader again and begin to prophesy unless given permission. This would be considered disorderly conduct. However, this may not be the protocol of your local assembly. Remember, it is according to the protocol of your house, which varies from church to church.

As a teacher, I encourage those that are just beginning to walk in this gift not to set people in offices when prophesying. For example, don't tell the person you are prophesying to that you hear the Lord saying you are a Prophet. No, we instead encourage by saying, "I see a prophetic anointing upon your life," or I hear the Lord saying, "that there is a strong prophetic calling upon your life." The reason for this is that you don't know where that person is in their walk with the Lord. That person may still be a babe in their Christian walk and you may choke them with this Word. I have been a witness of people who try to live up to prophetic Words spoken over their lives, without having all of the details of the making and processing that the Lord puts Prophets through before they begin to walk in the fullness of there callings. This goes for any ministry callings as well.

For example, I have received several Words that have not yet come to pass. I thought I was a failure when I would make a mistake or mess up in my attempt to live up to a prophetic Word spoken over my life. The truth is God was making me that I would be mature enough to carry the mantle and have enough character and integrity to fulfill the mandate with wisdom, grace, and the fruit of the Spirit being exhibited. I had a lot of work that needed to be done in my mind, will, emotions, character, and so forth. When delivering a prophetic Word, you should use wisdom in choosing your words and the Spirit in which you minister so you don't cause others to shipwreck.

On the other end of the spectrum, if a person knows that they are called, but refuses to submit this may be just the Word they were waiting for to fuel the fire of rebellion and cause them to run off and start their ministry prematurely. They may not shipwreck, but the process will take longer and they may have to endure more pressure that they could have avoided had they waited upon the Lord. Therefore, I encourage those who are not seasoned to leave the ministry callings to the leaders and presbytery staff chosen by leadership.

If your Word is judged, which it should be, then do not fret. Receive correction and God will honor you. A wise man receives correction and fools despise it. If you are innocent and falsely accused, you must let God be the judge and vindicator. Do not take matters into your own hands. Submit yourself and remember that God gives grace to the humble, but He resists the proud. You must never argue with your leaders, even if you are right and especially never in front of the assembly. It is disgraceful and dishonorable to behave this way.

I want to encourage you not to fall into witchcraft. Do not be sneaky and try to give Words behind the closed doors, through private notes, or by any other manner. You will be known as the little damsel in the Bible who spoke truth, but her motives were not pure (Acts 16:16, 17).

If possible, prophetic Words should be taped for the safety and integrity of the ministry. If anyone ever tries to say something was spoken over his or her lives and it is not true, then with a recording as a witness the ministry is safely protected. Another reason Words should be taped is because most people can't remember past the first two sentences. This way they have a point of reference, as well as encouragement during hard times. From time to time, I sit down and listen to the prophetic Words spoken over my life. It reminds me that no matter where I am in life, God has given me a bright future and I have hope (Jeremiah 29:11).

Chapter 3
PROCEDURES: DEVELOPING THE PROPHETIC GIFTING

ৡৣ

"For there is a proper time and procedure for every matter..."

(Ecclesiastes 8:6).

Procedures are the tell-tell teachings of how to conduct a matter. There can be several avenues and particular ways of accomplishing something. I want to show you a series of steps followed in a consistent, but diversified order that your Spirit may be trained to operate in this awesome gifting bestowed upon the Body of Christ by our heavenly Father. When you become seasoned or while you are maturing in this gifting, the Lord may show you some new methods. Like I said before, there are many avenues as long as you come to the same conclusion-You Can Prophesy!

1. <u>How to Become Sensitive and Hear the Voice of the Lord</u>

This is my favorite part- teaching others to hear the Master. One of my very dear friends, Mrs. Zianne, encouraged me to write down everything the Lord spoke to me. That was the greatest advice anyone has ever imparted into me. I began to journal every dream, revelation, Word of knowledge, Word of wisdom and even Words of correction from the Lord, which brought me to where I am now. I prophesy with skill and accuracy, not only from the teachings that I have received or the books and tapes full of knowledge that I have acquired, but also from journaling. This is one of the greatest tools to use to train your spirit to hear the voice of the Lord.

This is where the Lord trained me like he did David on the backside of the mountain. No one knew me, or what God had been doing in my life. I didn't even recognize what He was doing until the fullness of time came for me to be presented to the priest like David was to the prophet Samuel. It's funny now that I look back. I got the same reaction as King David. King David's father brought forth all of his sons before the prophet Samuel. David was not his father's first choice. My leader actually told me that he would never have picked me to be over the prophetic ministry because he thought I was "goofy and much too young," but the Lord told him to and so he did. Only God knew what was on the inside of me.

I want to encourage you to begin to write all of your feelings down. Be totally honest with the Lord because He knows our thoughts before we think them. There is no point in trying to hide your feelings. In your time of prayer, journal your thoughts, dreams, ideas, hopes, fears, feelings, inhibitions, failures, triumphs, and so forth, and remember to always allow God the opportunity to respond. This is the essence of journaling and developing sensitivity to hearing the Father's voice. Quiet yourself down, empty out all of your thoughts, and then let God respond.

Example:

Lord, I have been working on this book for sometime now and it is finally finished. I thank You for choosing me and giving me the boldness to step out and the ability to allow my wineskin to be renewed. Father, I thank You that I can receive the truth of the Word and embrace the fact that all of Your children can prophecy, if they so desire to covet this gift.

From God:

It was in you all of the time. I gave you the ability to hear and have a personal relationship with Me ever since the day I thought of you and My hands began to shape you. I set you within your mother's womb and I knew I could count on you to trust Me with blind faith and be all that I have called you to be.

2. <u>Become a Worshipper</u>

In praise and worship you are communing and communicating with the Heavenly Father. Worship is just an expression of how you feel about God with words accompanied by melody. You should still allow the Lord the opportunity to respond. God will sing back to you and fill you with words full of His love and adoration of you as His child. **"The Lord your God is with you, he is mighty to save. He will take great delight in you, he will quiet you with his love, he will rejoice over you with singing"** (**Zephaniah 3:17**). I once read a book by the name of God Chasers, but I have come to find that God chases after those who worship and praise Him. **"Yet a time is coming and has now come when the true worshippers will worship the Father in spirit and truth, for they are the kind of worshippers the Father seeks" (John 4: 23)**.

3. <u>Write Love Letters and Letters of Repentance</u>

Another strategy the Lord placed within my heart was to begin to write love letters and repentance letters to Him and I would allow Him to respond. The first few lines would be me, but eventually He would take over because of my faith. He met me where I was.

Example:

I love you Lord and You are my greatest asset; without You I could not make it in this life. You have done so much for me, and my family. I just want to say how thankful I am and I want to show my gratitude to You for the marvelous job You have done of reconstructing my broken heart. You have given me my own personal makeover and I appreciate You.

God:

I love you more than human words could ever express, and I have so much more for you. Just continue to put your trust in Me. When it seems as if the enemy has the upper hand, that is the time that you run to the secret place. Run to Me daughter, for I will never be the type of parent that is too busy to hear the cries of My children.

Me:

I don't know how to relate to You as a father because I have only had my mother. There was not a father figure in my life when I was growing up. I want to know You intimately, but I have a hard time being honest with my feelings because of all of the rejection and misunderstanding that I have suffered and had to endure. However, I know I love You and I want to be open towards You with my intimate feelings.

God:

That is the reason why I call you friend, because friends share and they learn to trust and work through their feelings with honesty. Don't worry. I love you regardless of what you do or feel. I am here for you and I will never leave you or betray you. I love you.

4. Study to Show Yourself Approved

Prophecy is speaking the Words of God so it is important that you be filled with His Word. Study the Word like it is the last book upon the earth. I used to read a lot of informational books and I still do. Books are good tools for acquiring knowledge, but there must be a balance if you are going to flow in the prophetic gifting. It is important to know the language, mannerisms, and characteristic traits of God.

5. Write the Word

As I began to study the Word of God in the beginning stages of my intimate walk with the Lord, another strategy He gave me was to write out the scriptures. As I wrote, the Lord would expound and explain them to me. I spent countless hours writing the Bible down word for word, and the Lord would give me illumination from His perspective concerning His word. I studied the Bible with a dictionary and a concordance nearby, but it got to the point that the

Holy Spirit would answer the questions in my mind before I could search for the answers.

6.   Prophesy Rhema from the Logos

Another example of using scripture to train your spirit is actually by prophesying the scripture. This was great training because I would stand before the people and the Lord would quicken a scripture from my spiritual archive.

Example:

"Therefore if anyone be in Christ, he is a new creation; the old has gone, the new has come" (2 Corinthians 5:17)! It is Me that has given you a new identity and washed away the reproach that has stained you because of the sins of your past. You are made brand new- a new creation. The odor from sin has been cleansed by My son's blood. The old is gone and now the new has come.

Example:

"Being confident of this, that he that began the good work in you will carry it on to completion to the day of Christ Jesus" (Philippians 1:6). My daughter/son, the good work that I have began in you I am now fine tuning it and you are beginning to see the calling upon your life more clearly. Do not fret or be intimidated because I am with you every step of the way and I will

make sure that what I have destined for you will be completed.

You can prophesy scripture over your life everyday and watch your hearing become more and more sensitive to the Holy Spirit as He releases the mind of Christ upon you.

7.   Practice on Your Family

If your family allows you to, practice on them every chance you get. I prophesy over my children, husband, the cat, finances, job etc. You can use all of these techniques to begin to be developed for precision accuracy when delivering a prophetic Word. Don't forget the safety zone when practicing on others (1 Corinthians 14:3). Under no circumstances should you rebuke, or release words of correction without a seasoned leader to judge your Words when practicing on others. Always be cognizant and respectful to the protocol of your local assembly. If you prophesy without a covering, you are headed for trouble. The enemy is lurking and waiting for you to enter into the spirit realm illegally.

8. Practice by Writing Prophetic Prayers

I used to write prophetic prayers to my peers and email them. The response I would get was phenomenal. This is different from a prophetic Word; it is prophetic prayer. If there is no training at your church in the prophetic gifting then allow God to enroll you into the school of the Holy Spirit. These are just a few ways you can allow your spirit to become sensitive and recognize the voice of the Lord. Have fun with the Lord. Although this book is about you coming into the knowledge of being used by God to deliver a prophetic Word, it is also about you hearing the voice of God for yourself. Scripture says God's sheep know His voice. Knowing (recognizing) and hearing the voice of God is what every believer has the ability to do. I pray the Lord pours out His Spirit upon you as you go forth in this precious ability given to the Body of Christ.

9. <u>Pray, Pray, Pray and Pray</u>

It is imperative that you cultivate and develop an intimate relationship with the Lord through prayer. His sheep may know His voice, but does He know your voice? **"Many will say to me on that day, Lord, Lord, have we not prophesied in your name? And in thy name have cast out devils? And in thy name done many wonderful works? And then will I profess unto them, I never knew you: depart from me, ye that work iniquity" (Matthew 7: 22, 23).** A prophetic personality without a strong disciplined prayer life is an accident waiting to happen. You must commune with the Heavenly Father if you are to properly represent His kingdom as a prophetic Ambassador. May God bless you and keep you in His perfect will as you develop in the prophetic gifting.

YOU CAN PROPHESY!

All About The Author
Charmein T. Downer

&Q&

Born the eldest of three children to Joycelyn McCormick-Davis, Prophetess. Downer comes from a legacy of pastors, preachers, intercessors, and singers. She is currently attending Destiny School of Ministry Bible College in Lansing, Michigan where she is working on her Bachelors' Degree in Theology. She is an active member of Lakeshore International Family Training Center under the leadership of Pastors Jeffrie and Maria Hunter.

Charmein has a strong apostolic mantle on her life for deliverance and is a demon-buster called to set the captives free. She has a passion to pioneer unchartered territories in the Spirit as a trailblazer for her generation. Prophetess Downer is an end-time Prophet with a strong teaching anointing to help the people of God walk in their purpose and identity, and demonstrate the power of God with authority. She flows heavily in both spiritual warfare and prophetic intercession. With a mandate from God, she is a wise master builder skilled in training teams in the prophetic intercession.

Her grace gift is to recognize and activate spiritual gifts that are lying dormant on the inside of God's people. Prophetess Downer is God's mouthpiece chosen for this dispensation of time to release revelation knowledge and present-day truth that will upgrade and thrust the Body of Christ into new dimensions of the Spirit.

She has been married to her husband, George Downer for thirteen years and is the mother of four children (Aaron, Chanae, Chantae, and Cimone). Prophetess Downer has a heart for seeing the Body of Christ restored to its rightful positions. As we fulfill the prophetic Word spoken in Genesis and take our place ruling, subduing, and having dominion once again in the earth, we remind satan that God is still in control and on the throne.

For speaking engagements, workshops, and seminars, she can be contacted by e-mail:

Prophetess Charmein Downer
Email: chosen2beavessel@yahoo.com

Printed in the United States
73058LV00002B/1-75